Joanna Thompson

Season of Love

Thienemann

Wolke 8

Where am I right now, exactly? I'm on the London Eye, of course, the biggest **ferris wheel** in Europe. I'm kissing Sam, high above London. I'm ecstatic, so in German I'm on *Wolke 7*. In English, I'm even happier, a bit higher – on *Cloud 9*.

My question is this: if you're ecstatic and bilingual like me, then which cloud/Wolke am I on – number 8? It's just a thought, of course. It doesn't really matter. Wherever Sam and me are now, we're in love heaven. It's a perfect day, there's not another cloud in the sky.

But wait! Aha! *Of course* there is! Firstly because this is *England* and there must be more than one cloud in the sky. It's the law or something. And secondly, well, because this is *life* and there are permanently clouds everywhere, hanging out and waiting to rain on your happiness. You know the kind of clouds I mean. Oh yes.

Sam and me aren't kissing anymore. We're not even talking. We're just holding hands, **gazing** out at London and the sky above it. Our happiness can't really **last**. We

+++ ferris wheel – Riesenrad +++ to gaze – schauen +++ to last – andauern, halten +++

know that. We're both looking at our own personal clouds on the horizon.

There's mine, I can see it now. A normal cloud, at first sight, perfect and **fluffy**, really **innocent**. "Trust me!" it seems to say. "Rain all over you? No way! I'm a sunny-day-sort-of-cloud." That's when you notice that though this cloud *looks* white, it's actually a nasty dark grey colour. And it's *moving into your* ***dorm***.

Meet my "cloud" – Amanda "**Cyclops**" Dobson. My big-eyed new roommate. There will have to be a bit of cloudbusting in dorm 3B later, I think. Right now, I'm more worried about Sam's cloud.

Sam. Sam Reid, I've just learned. Sam is the drummer with the Kitty Gagarins, the band from St Dougan's boys' school. He's also **gorgeous**. I was blind to that fact at first – oh! – and instead fell in love with, oh, here he comes now, floating over towards us. A **floppy-haired** cloud, which looks a bit angry and is holding an electric guitar.

Why, it's Ed Stanton! Guitarist and super Blogger (a.D.). He broke my heart, of course, **dumping** me by text. And I soon learned I was not what you'd call Ed's one and only love. This was very easy to find out, in fact – Ed had helpfully set up a website, telling the whole of cyberspace what he'd done to me. Maudie and Kim, my new friends waiting down below right now, were also his **victims**. He dumped them, too, after relation-

+++ fluffy – flauschig +++ innocent – unschuldig +++ dorm – Schlafsaal +++ cyclops – Zyklop +++ gorgeous – wunderschön +++ floppy-haired – mit wuscheligen Haaren +++ to dump – Schluss machen +++ victim – Opfer +++

ships that lasted as long as a litre of milk left in the sun. Brutal.

But we three girls decided that enough was enough and that Ed's "Babe Blog" had to be stopped. We had some help with this from Sam, which explains why he's now looking so worried.

Sam hasn't just got great rhythm and beautiful, peaceful blue eyes. He's also a computer genius. It was him who designed a website for us that made Ed look *soooo* stupid. It was the perfect **revenge**. We were so proud. But now, it seems, Sam's in danger. There's a rock 'n' roll rainstorm coming.

If Ed finds out that Sam helped us, he could make Sam's life miserable. Ed could get Sam kicked out of the band. And if Ed sees Sam and me kissing and holding hands, it won't take him long to work things out, will it?

+++ revenge – Rache +++

We're nearly back in Britain. The London Eye is swinging round towards **terra firma**. Sam and me look at each other. He **blushes**. I blush. One of us has to speak. *Has to.*

Sam's staring at his shoes, a very nice pair of Nike Uptowns. It's going to have to be me who breaks the silence, I see. "So, what now?" I say quietly. Maudie and Kim are waiting for us and I'm not sure how to act in front of them. Are they allowed to know that Sam and me have just kissed? Or is it better to say nothing and play it cool?

Sam's eyes don't move from his shoes. "Let's just keep things quiet for the moment, eh?" he **mumbles**. "I really want to be with you. I just need a bit of time to think about how to play things. I wasn't expecting this today. But I've liked you for ages, you know that."

Ages! I could *kick* myself. Why couldn't I have noticed Sam first? *Why?* I'm so stupid.

"It's fine," I say quickly to Sam. Quickly because I believe him and quickly because it's time to jump from the London Eye now. The ground is **rushing** up …

Geronimo!! We're off. We **glance** around for a second – Maudie and Kim are nowhere to be seen. Sam gives my hand a last squeeze and then lets it go. We walk off together, trying to look friendly, but not too friendly. Relaxed.

It takes us a couple of minutes of walking in a

+++ terra firma – feste Erde +++ to blush – rot werden +++ to mumble – murmeln +++ to rush – hier: sich nähern +++ to glance – schauen +++

friendly, relaxed **manner** to find Maudie and Kim. They're standing next to a wall by the river, watching the boats that carry tourists up and down the Thames. They wave at us enthusiastically and Sam and me wander over and join them. We are masters of discretion. We can do this undercover love thing, I'm sure of it.

Kim's very scared of heights, which is why she and Maudie didn't make the trip on the Eye with us. I think, in her heart, Kim wasn't even expecting us to come back alive. She throws her arms around me, emotionally, as though I'd just returned from K2.

"How was it?" grins Maudie, when Kim finally lets go of me. It's a bit of a cheeky grin, actually. Hmmm. Has she noticed something?

I'm trying really hard not to smile myself. I shrug my shoulders. "It was OK," I say, **casually**. "Nothing too exciting."

Nothing too exciting! The kiss of a lifetime and yet I still actually manage to sound like I've just been round a museum of farming **tools** with my grandma, the Queen Mother. *Genius.* Sam's doing well, too, **yawning** and looking at his watch. Bored!

I'm not going to lie to Maudie and Kim about Sam, of course – **no way**. I saw what happened when my ex-**roommate** Olga lied to Melissa, my still-roommate. (That's *why* Olga's now my ex-roommate, of course.) But I *do* just want to give Sam a chance to work out a plan of action.

+++ manner – Art und Weise +++ casually – beiläufig +++ tools – Werkzeug +++ to yawn – gähnen +++ no way – auf keinen Fall +++ roommate – Mitbewohner/in +++

I'm feeling really pleased with my "performance" when, out of the corner of my eye, I notice a large man waving at the four of us. I've no idea who he is, so I look away quickly. London is full of crazy people – "nutters" they call them here. I'm a magnet for them. They're always stopping me and asking whether I've seen Napoleon or George Clooney anywhere.

The man hasn't given up and is still signalling wildly at us. Sam's **spotted** him, too, now. He makes a worried face. "You know him?"

"No," I mumble, though I am *sort of* thinking that I have seen the man's face somewhere before. Then – disaster! – the man opens his mouth and **roars**,

"Oooiii! Romeo and Juliet! You two lovebirds!"

Oh Lordy! It's too late but now *I really do* remember. Shouting Man was sitting opposite us in the London Eye! Oh, *it can't be.* He's coming over and he's carrying my camera! I actually left my camera in the Eye!

Sam and me look at each other, horrified. Shouting Man is standing next to us now, holding my beloved Pentax in his hands. He's middle-aged, with quite a large **belly**. He looks a bit angry. It's no wonder – we've been rolling our eyes and acting like he's a **lunatic**.

"You two were too busy kissing to remember this, eh?" It's his turn to roll his eyes. "You should watch your stuff more carefully. You were lucky."

I manage to mumble *thank you* to him. My hands are shaking – imagine if I'd lost my *camera.* It would be like

+++ to spot – sehen +++ to roar – brüllen +++ belly – Bauch +++ lunatic – Verrückte/r +++

losing a **lung** or something. I'm so hot in the face now you could fry chips on me and serve them at White Out, our favourite café. Undercover love, eh? If I were a spy, I'd just have been shot.

I can't look at anyone, not at Sam, nor the girls. Finally Maudie bursts out laughing.

"Kim, pay up. You owe me five pounds."

Kim laughs, too, and actually gets her purse, a pink **leather** one with a small frog on the front, from the pocket of her jeans. She takes out a five-pound note. "Maudie, you're good," she says admiringly.

Maudie smiles proudly. "I bet Kim that you two would have a little kiss up there. I could *smell* the hormones. Keeping it a secret from us, were you?"

"No," says Sam, before I can open my mouth. His voice is very firm, almost **statesmanlike**. I feel strangely relieved that he sounds so sure. "Absolutely not. I just need to **figure out** what to do about Ed first."

Everyone goes quiet. Ed – the **tie** that binds us all. To us girls, he might be the floppy-haired, guitar-playing devil but he's still Sam's friend. And the Kitty Gagarins are a great band. It would be terrible if they split up.

"We're **supposed to** have our first day in a recording studio soon," mumbles Sam. "I mean, if I could at least keep things with Emily quiet till after then it would be good."

+++ lung – Lungenflügel +++ leather – Leder +++ statesmanlike – staatsmännisch +++ to figure out – sich überlegen +++ tie – Band +++ to be supposed to do sth. – etwas tun sollen +++

The day in the studio is approaching, I suddenly remember. The Kitty Gagarins want to record their first single – "Too Cool for School" – there. Ed's dad is paying for the session. Paying *a lot of money* for the session.

Everyone looks deep in thought for a moment, as though they were **digging** in their brains for ideas. Silence. No one seems to have any brilliant suggestions about what to do about Ed. Then Maudie waves her five-pound note and says brightly, "Hot chocolate anyone? Now that I'm rich."

Five pounds won't buy us four plastic **lids** in this part of London, of course, but we all **head off** towards a coffee stand which Maudie's spotted. Sam suddenly grabs my hand: "Nothing to hide here anymore, have we?"

All too soon, it starts to get dark – those clouds, remember! – and it's time to head back to school. Chalk Farm School for Girls for the ladies, St Dougan's Boys' School for Sam.

I say a quick goodbye to Sam at the gates of Chalk Farm. He'll call me, he says, giving me a soft kiss. The **weird** thing is that I'm sure he means it. After the whole horrible Ed affair, I should be worried or nervous but I'm not. I know that Sam will phone me because he's normal and nice. *Punkt.* I don't even need *Bettis Top-Liebestest* to tell me that. (But yes, Betti, if you're reading this, Sam *does* look back at me as he heads off to St Dougan's.)

+++ to dig – graben +++ lid – Deckel +++ to head off – losziehen +++ weird – komisch +++

Maudie and Kim wait till Sam's gone and then explode. They can't stop talking about how *great/wonderful/fabulous* they think it is that Sam and me are together.

"Oooh, he's lovely, *nothing* like Ed," says Maudie firmly.

Kim sighs a lot and nods. "*Nothing,*" she repeats.

Then it's off the girls go, back to Bloomsbury, one of Chalk Farm school's four houses. I'm jealous, of course. Bloomsbury's full of lovely, cool creative girls. And I'm in Kensington, which isn't. It's the "House of Horror" with its very own in-house witch, Cyclops Dobson.

My heart finally sinks. It's been paragliding after the perfect afternoon with Sam and now it crash lands, here on the stairs back up to the dorm. I stop. Oh man, I really don't want to see Amanda right now. I could go to the **common room**, hang out there for a bit …

But hurrah! Call it karma, call it bad luck – Amanda "Cyclops" Dobson is already in the common room, lying on the sofa, sunglasses on her head, as usual! I should have remembered. It's Saturday night. Or as it's known in our house: *Windswept Love* night.

Windswept Love is a TV soap that half the girls in Kensington are crazy about. I saw it once and nearly **vomited** my whole stomach out. The show tells the story of a **handsome** young **vet** who moves to the English countryside and falls in love with a **widow** who has six cute children. It's *terrible.* Your *Oma* wouldn't watch *Windswept Love*, not even if you *swore* that Götz George

+++ common room – Aufenthaltsraum +++ to vomit – sich übergeben +++ handsome – gut aussehend +++ vet – Tierarzt +++ widow – Witwe +++

was in it. But there's a gang of brain-dead girls who always meet here to watch it, mostly members of Amanda's clique.

They're a weird **bunch**, Amanda's gang – a bit like the Addams Family in school uniforms. There's Laurie, Amanda's so-called "best friend". She won't wear glasses and can't wear contact lenses, so she never makes eye contact with you because she can't find your eyes. She's not the strangest member of "Team Cyclops", though, oh no.

The strangest members, I've discovered, are a pair of identical twins – Florence and Sienna. I'm actually a bit scared of identical twins if I'm honest. This pair never speak, not even to each other and always look as though they've just finished a week of electric shock **treatment**. I have no idea which twin is which, though Melissa told me once that Sienna has a much deeper voice than Florence. The spooky twins are actually in Knightsbridge House but they *always* seem to be with Cyclops.

Windswept Love's just starting as I enter the room – it has a horrible **theme tune**, all tearful violins. I look around in terror. I must escape! I try to **sneak** back out again but Amanda's seen me. That big old eye of hers misses nothing. "Oh, it's Emily the Strange, my new sleeping partner. How wonderful!"

Sleeping partner? *Ugh*. And "Emily the Strange" – how very original.

Amanda nods at the television where I can see the

+++ bunch – Haufen +++ treatment – Behandlung +++ theme tune – Erkennungsmelodie +++ to sneak – schleichen +++

handsome vet listening to a sheep's heart. "Why don't you join us, darling? I can explain things to you if there's something you don't understand."

She's always doing this, Amanda, acting like I'm an idiot because I have two first languages. She talks to me in a stupid voice too – really s-l-o-w-l-y. It drives me *crazy.*

"No thanks," I mutter, "**not my cup of tea**. I wanted to watch that documentary about **al-Qaeda** on the other channel tonight." It's a **plain lie**, of course. Laurie gives me a funny look. She probably thinks al-Qaeda is a boy band.

Windswept Love is now really getting going – *that sheep's not going to make it!* Amanda can't decide whether to annoy me some more or concentrate on the show. She decides to have one last piece of fun.

"I'm all moved into the dorm, darling," she **trills**, without taking her eyes off the TV. "So, I'll see you in about an hour? Maybe I can read you a bedtime story?"

Laurie and the spooky twins **giggle**.

"Great," I mumble, turning to leave. I'm so out of here.

+++ not my cup of tea – nicht mein Ding +++ al-Qaeda – Al Kaida +++ plain lie – glatte Lüge +++ to trill – flöten +++ to giggle – kichern +++

Pimp My Dorm

I'm not happy. And I'm about to get even less happy. I'm half-way along the corridor, walking back to the dorm, when I see it: one of the bedside tables from our room, sitting outside the door. The little table has a large orange label on it: *Please take to cellar.* That's a bit odd, I think. Then I open the door.

Ta Dah! I can only guess that the crazy guy from *Pimp My Ride* has **teamed up with** that big blonde woman from *Einsatz in vier Wänden* and broken into dorm 3B while I've been away. *What on earth?*

I rub my eyes, hard. Harder. Amanda will sleep in Olga's old bed now and I **suppose** it must be the same one. It's hard to tell, though – the bed's now covered in a **silky**-looking, **pale** pink **blanket**, instead of the plain grey ones we all have. And it must be what was Olga's bedside table sitting outside the door. In its place there's a large dark wood antique **dresser**. It takes up half the room.

It gets worse. On the wall above Amanda's new bed

+++ to pimp – aufmotzen +++ to team up with s.o. – sich mit jmdm. zusammentun +++ to suppose – annehmen +++ silky – seidig +++ pale – blass +++ blanket – Decke +++ dresser – Frisierkommode +++

hangs a gold-framed photo of a baby dressed up as a **fairy**. It's *disgusting*. I'd rather have a life-sized picture of Angela Merkel in a bikini smiling down at me.

The icing on the cake is a horrible sheepskin **rug** that now almost completely covers our lovely wooden floorboards. I'm going to **trip** over that at least 20 times a day, I can just *feel* it.

I'm shocked. Everyone – and I mean *everyone* – at Chalk Farm School has exactly the same *everything*. We all wear the same terrible clothes, our **burgundy** and yellow uniforms. We eat the same **dreadful** food, **chewy beef olives** and potatoes that break your teeth. We sleep under the same **itchy** bed covers, sit on the same uncomfortable chairs. We're miserable clones, really. We are each other.

+++ fairy – Fee +++ the icing on the cake – *hier:* die Krönung +++ rug – Teppich +++ to trip – stolpern +++ burgundy – burgunderrot +++ dreadful – schrecklich +++ chewy – zäh +++ beef olives – Rindsroulade +++ itchy – kratzig +++

Miss Bardwell, our housemistress and Latin teacher, once told me that this was because we're all part of the same team: no one here is different, no one is special. But it seems I must have misheard her. It seems what Miss Bardwell actually said was – no one here is different or special *except* Amanda Dobson, her pet. Miss Bardwell loves Amanda. They're blackhearted **soulmates**.

I'm standing frozen in the doorway, just staring at what used to be dorm 3B, when I hear a **cough**. I notice for the first time that Melissa and Becks, my two human roommates, are actually in the dorm, too, playing cards on Melissa's bed. Melissa's eyes follow mine and land, nervously, on Amanda's corner of the room. Becks and Melissa know that I didn't want Cyclops here in our dorm.

Melissa giggles. She's horse crazy, but actually surprisingly nice **in spite of** that. "Right, well, yes. Amanda's made a *couple* of little changes. She's allergic to the school blankets, apparently. She has to have Egyptian cotton sheets with a 400 **thread count** or her bad eye gets really **sore**."

Her bad eye. Amanda was hit by a hockey ball *years* ago and one eye is slightly bigger than the other – **hence** the nickname Cyclops. I'm no doctor but I can't imagine that eyes are sensitive to *thread count.* Why can't that diva be allergic to **oxygen** or something?

And, personally, giant pictures of babies make *my*

+++ soulmate – Seelenverandte/r +++ cough – Husten +++ in spite of – trotzdem +++ thread count – Fadenzahl +++ sore – wund, schlimm +++ hence – daher +++ oxygen – Sauerstoff +++

eyes water and my skin itch. No one cares about that. "And the dresser??" I **gasp**. There are rules. Rules. *No personal furniture.*

Melissa nods uncertainly. "It belonged to Amanda's grandmother and she died recently. Amanda's therapist said she should have something of her grandmother's around to help her get over the pain."

Amanda's *therapist.* It's unbelievable – and so unfair. We *share* the dorm. Why should Amanda be allowed to pimp up *our* space? Why should I have to live with her horrible things?

Becks, our **resident** muscular sports monster, laughs nervously. "Not to worry, eh, Emily?" she booms. "I quite like it all. Bit different, eh? And at least …"

Becks doesn't finish her sentence. I'm sure she had been about to say: *at least Olga's gone*, but the official dorm 3B policy is not to talk about Olga anymore. I think it's too painful for Melissa – she misses Olga, I know she does.

"We'll get used to it," says Melissa bravely. I'm sure that I can smell her **doubt**, though. Or maybe it's just the **scent** of the giant orange candle, **roughly** the size of the *Fernsehturm* in Berlin, which Amanda has put on top of her wardrobe.

Enough already. I give up. Bathroom and sleep. But the nightmare continues. I walk into our shared bathroom and, ooh, guess what? *Come in and find out*: Douglas have apparently opened a **branch** in Chalk Farm

+++ to gasp – nach Luft schnappen +++ resident – ortsansässig +++ doubt – Zweifel +++ scent – Geruch +++ roughly – ungefähr +++ branch – Zweigstelle +++

School for Girls. There are now about six hundred bottles and **jars** packed onto our tiny shelves – toner, **cleanser**, special deep cleanser, anti-acne cream, special deep anti-acne cream. And about 20 different eye products: eye gel, eye balm, eye cooler, eye cream.

I can't believe any of this is really happening. I feel like banging my head against the wall.

It's Monday. 7.02 am in the dorm and I discover that Amanda is not just so "special" that she needs her own furniture and blankets. She's generally so "**unique**," it seems, that she doesn't have to get out of bed when the rest of us do. By some miracle, Cyclops even manages to sleep through the rising bell. This is the bell which rings to wake us every morning and it's *loud* – it's a bit like having Big Ben **strike** seven *in* your face.

We've all showered and have our uniforms on and Amanda is *still* asleep. It's then that I prove to everyone in dorm 3B that I actually have **supernatural** powers.

I'm trying to get to my school bag when I trip over the stupid, ugly rug lying in the middle of the floor. (See, I knew I would fall over it. I **predicted** I would a few pages earlier, remember? I *can* tell the future. I'll be seeing dead people next.) I **stumble** and land near Amanda's bed, actually waking her up.

Amanda doesn't think there's anything either "super" or "natural" about what's just happened. She's actually

+++ jar – Töpfchen +++ cleanser – Reinigungsmilch +++ unique – einzigartig +++ to strike – schlagen +++ supernatural – übernatürlich +++ to predict – vorhersagen +++ to stumble – stolpern +++

angry at me for having interrupted her "beauty sleep". She sits up in bed, **scowling** under her blue eye **patch**. She growls deeply, "Emily Elephant – my God, what a noise!"

Elephant? I can't help it, I'm ***furious***. "I didn't put the stupid rug here!" I shout. "And, anyway, the rising bell's already rung or are you **deaf** as well as …"

Blind. That's the last word of the sentence. *Deaf as well as blind.* I stop myself, just in time, and don't actually say it. Melissa gasps, then runs from the room with a worried-faced Becks. *Englische Feiglinge.*

Amanda looks at me in horror but I don't care. I grab my school bag and leave the dorm. Secretly, of course, I'm glad I didn't say *blind.* It would have been a pretty **bitchy** thing to say. *If* I had said it. But I didn't. So it's fine. Right?

There's been yet another change in dorm 3B – a statistical one. **It used to always be** the case that 100% of the dorm hated going to Latin on Monday mornings. This number has now fallen to 75%. 25% of dorm 3B now love Latin. They *love* being with someone who *loves* them.

When 75% of the dorm – the nice part, Melissa, Becks and me – arrive in Latin that morning, the other (horrible) 25% is already there, talking to Miss Bardwell. Amanda's body language says clearly that she wants something. Miss Bardwell is listening carefully to Amanda. *Her* body language says clearly: *Amanda, I love*

+++ to scowl – finster blicken +++ patch – Augenklappe +++ furious – wütend +++ deaf – taub +++ bitchy – gehässig +++ It used to always be … – Es war immer … +++

*you. I will hunt down and **punish** anyone who is nasty to you.*

I keep one eye on the two of them – Miss Bardwell and Amanda are the enemy and must always be watched – but I'm actually more interested in Olga. She's sitting near the back of the room and I'm **wondering** how she'll react to seeing Melissa, Becks and myself. I'm wasting my time. Olga doesn't even *look* at any of us as we come in. We don't exist anymore, apparently. We're the invisible three from dorm 3B.

Amanda is now back in her seat and Miss Bardwell is ready to begin. She's tapping the desk impatiently with her **claws**, sorry, elegant long fingernails. Today is a slightly more interesting start to Latin than the usual "Festina, serve!" nonsense: "Firstly, girls, an announcement about the Kensington Christmas party."

It's November and only five weeks until Christmas. Each house at Chalk Farm School organizes its own Christmas party. My **amazing** supernatural powers tell me that the Kensington party is not going to be the *wildest* one ever. I don't think the common room television will be thrown into the school swimming pool.

I'm right. Miss Bardwell goes through the programme: *The Kensington party will be held in the assembly hall, on Saturday 22nd of December, between 4 and 7 pm. Pupils are allowed to bring a maximum of two guests, family members only please. Games will be played and soft drinks and **mince pies** served.*

+++ to punish – bestrafen +++ to wonder – sich fragen +++ claw – Kralle, Klaue +++ amazing – erstaunlich +++ mince pie – süßes Weihnachtsgebäck +++

Wow! *Cool.* I'd say there's a pretty good chance Pete Doherty and Amy Winehouse will leave their Camden **crack dens** – just up the road! Maudie told me! – and come over to Kensington House that night. *Rock 'n' roll.*

Miss Bardwell is still going through all the "highlights": "And a certain gentleman in a red coat may stop by and pay us a visit."

Sadie, the *Intelligenzbestie* in our class, gasps excitedly, "Santa!" Someone else **groans.** *Santa.* We're *teenagers!*

Miss Bardwell's finished telling us about the party and is now talking about the genitive singular. I drift off. Christmas. I wonder – Berlin or London this year? It's not yet clear. My mum really wants to be here in England, with the Queen Mother and possibly my Auntie Nora at The Grange, Grandma's big house.

My father, however, wants to have *Weihnachten in Berlin*, the official centre of the **universe**, eating *Heringssalat* and watching *Loriot* **repeats** with his brother, my weird Onkel Dieter. Deep down, I think my father is scared. He's scared of a repeat of 2001.

2001 was the last year we spent Christmas in England and a total *disaster.* There were massive *kulturelle Missverständnisse*, like my father saying, casually, at dinner on the 25th of December that he "always preferred **goose** to **turkey**".

Understand this: my grandmother has her turkey **hand reared** at a local farm. She even gives her turkey a

+++ crack den – Crack-Bude +++ to groan – stöhnen +++ universe – Universum +++ repeat – Wiederholung +++ goose – Gans +++ turkey – Truthahn +++ hand reared – von Hand aufgezogen +++

name – that year it was "Daphne", I remember – and goes to visit it twice a week. It costs a **fortune**; keeping Daphne alive till December was probably about as expensive as sending me to school in London. And there's my father on Christmas Day, looking at Daphne's **remains** like they were sugar-coated beef olives.

The meal was over. The holiday was over. We haven't spent Christmas here on the Island since. But this year, my mother has bravely decided that we should try again. The Queen Mother never comes to Berlin – she's 83 now and she can't live forever. Even though my father claims that my grandma is *unsterblich*, my mother knows that she's probably not.

I'm not sure what I want to do. On the one hand, I'd quite like to spend Christmas here, especially if Auntie Nora can make it. Auntie Nora is totally coolio. We can talk about photography, which we both love, and I can tell her all about Sam! On the other hand, I'd love to see Betti and Merle and *Berlin*. Have a *Milchkaffee* in *Mondstein* and hang out. I could tell *them* all about Sam!

Latin is almost finished. I haven't listened to a thing today! Oh well, Melissa always listens. She can let me know what the homework is. I pack up my bag and I'm just about to tap Melissa on the shoulder when Miss Bardwell says **tensely**: "Emily, I'd like just five minutes of your time, please."

Melissa looks at me sympathetically. Then she – and everyone else – disappears. I'm alone.

+++ fortune – Vermögen +++ remains – Überreste +++ tense – angespannt +++

If you had had a **lobotomy** that had gone very wrong and you actually *liked* Miss Bardwell, you *might* say that she reminded you of *Schneewittchen*, with her dark, dark hair and white, white skin. Myself, I see her more as a vampire. It doesn't help that teachers here wear long Batman-style black **gowns**. She looks super **creepy** today. Sort of like Marilyn Manson with a **hangover**.

Miss Bardwell shows me her pointed teeth – not really a smile, more of an **enamel**-based **threat**. "You know exactly why you're here, I suppose …"

I think for a moment. I can't, honestly, think of anything really terrible that I've done. Not this week. I mean, I wasn't totally listening in class, is it that? I'm starting to wish this was *Wer wird Millionär*? and I could phone a friend. I'd call Betti, of course. *Betti, ganz schnell, warum stehe ich hier? Was hab ich getan? Betti? Betti??*

But there are no lifelines today. Miss Bardwell comes straight to the point: "You're not making your new roommate feel welcome, I hear. You made a comment about her eyesight this morning, is that true?" Miss Bardwell's face is *furious*.

My heart sinks – I suppose I *did* ask Amanda if she were deaf. But not blind! I didn't say blind!

"I won't stand for any jokes about another pupil's **disability**, is that clear? Amanda's eye injury has caused her endless …"

+++ lobotomy – Hirn-OP, bei der Nervenbahnen durchtrennt werden +++ gown – Umhang, Kittel +++ creepy – gruselig +++ hangover – Kater +++ enamel – Zahnschmelz +++ threat – Drohung +++ disability – Behinderung +++

Disability – ha! It's a microscopic cosmetic **flaw**! Amanda's not exactly going to qualify for the Paralympics. And I seem to remember hearing Cyclops, I mean Amanda, being pretty bitchy to Moira, the girl in our house who's in a wheelchair and is, like, *really disabled.*

I'm trying to interrupt now and tell Miss Bardwell that I didn't make a joke about Amanda's *eyes* but about her *ears*, but Miss Bardwell doesn't seem to hear me. She's deaf, too!

Instead she says, stiffly, "We had a disappointing **incident** a couple of weeks ago with the essay, Emily. Please remember that I will be writing your report cards for this **term** in the next few weeks."

Ooh, power, she loves it.

She's got me, of course. Report cards. *Schulzeugnisse.* Great. Just imagine – the Queen Mother spends the **GDP** of Mexico to send me to Chalk Farm School and I get a report card saying something like: *Emily is useless and should just go home.*

I'm free to go, but it's ***depressing.*** It's like I've got the words "*Punish me, I'm bad*" tattooed on my **forehead.** I can't help but think that when Miss Bardwell looks at me, she sees my Auntie Nora. Miss Bardwell and Auntie Nora were at school together at Chalk Farm years ago; they hated each other. Nora told me that Miss Bardwell's love of my grandmother – and her money – would pro-

+++ flaw – Defekt, Makel +++ incident – Vorfall +++ term – Schulhalbjahr +++ GDP (gross domestic product) – BIP (Bruttoinlandsprodukt) +++ depressing – deprimierend +++ forehead – Stirn +++

tect me. But it seems money actually *can't* buy me Miss Bardwell's love.

Hmmm. I'm beginning to have a lovely idea, though. We're allowed to invite two family members to the Christmas party, eh? I think I've just decided who to put on my guest list. I'll call Nora tonight!

The rest of the day is more positive. The good thing about winter, **apart from** Christmas, is that there are *no more field sports.* Hockey **RIP**! Instead we have nice, gentle, indoor sports – like my personal favourite, table tennis. Fantastic. We're playing that today. I'm actually OK at it and I shock Becks by winning my first game against her. Becks is a truly good sport, though, and we're just having a laugh about my victory when: *ping pong! Zickenalarm!* I spot Amanda coming over to our table.

She's not playing today, Cyclops – period pains, apparently. She gets her period four times a month, as far as I can make out. Perhaps it's because of her eye.

"Did Miss Bardwell have a word with you then, Emily?" She smiles her serpent's smile. I bet she's secretly a bilingual, too – English and Parseltongue. Ha!

"Yup," I reply, scowling at her. "She said you're a special needs child and I should be nice to you."

Becks actually laughs. (In Britain, *special needs children = Kinder mit sonderpädagogischen Bedürfnissen.* This is why she laughs.)

Amanda turns to face Becks now. Becks goes pale,

+++ apart from – neben, außer +++ RIP = rest in peace – Ruhe in Frieden +++

even though she's built like a bus and 15 times Amanda's size. Amanda makes her nervous, with good reason.

"At least you laugh quieter than you **snore**, Becks. My goodness, I thought the ghost of the Titanic had docked in our bedroom last night. Honk! Honk!" Amanda **snorts**.

Becks is bright red. It's true, she does snore, and loudly. I've sort of got used to it – Melissa usually wears **earplugs**.

Amanda hasn't finished with poor Becks yet. She can't stop. "Have you considered **surgery**, Becks? Perhaps we could collect money for it?"

I say quickly, "Funny how you couldn't hear the rising bell this morning but you did hear Becks snoring …" Then I stop. Amanda's probably wearing a microphone and Miss Bardwell will be sitting in her office upstairs, like the Stasi officer in *Das Leben der Anderen.* She'll be listening to our conversation, just waiting for me to tell Amanda that she's a *big-eyed loser* so she can jump out of hiding and take me to a **damp** cellar and **beat me up**. So I say *nothing.*

+++ to snore – schnarchen +++ to snort – schnauben +++ earplugs – Ohrstöpsel +++ surgery – chirurgischer Eingriff +++ damp – feucht +++ to beat s.o. up – jmdn. zusammenschlagen +++

Emily the Exorcist

I say nothing, more or less, for the rest of the day. Today's one of those days when it just seems like an excellent idea to keep my mouth shut. Anyway, my mouth will – I hope – need all its energy for my romantic rendezvous with Sam in White Out later.

I love White Out. It's actually the place where I had my first date with Ed Stanton, but I've forgiven it for that. It's a great old traditional English café where they serve **greasy** fish and chips and greasy cups of tea and they call you "dearie". I've even brought my camera with me tonight, so I can get some pictures of some greasy **locals**. And I might take a couple of pictures of Sam, of course. Well, he is totally photogenic. I've got three films with me!

I can see him through the window now as I hurry along Chalk Farm Road. He's on time, as usual, and has got a brilliant table.

I've run all the way here so as not to be too late. Betti always told me never to be early for a date – *sieht verzweifelt aus*! Luckily, I find that an easy rule to stick

+++ exorcist – Teufelsaustreiber/in +++ greasy – fettig +++ local – Einheimische/r +++

to. I sit down, still **panting**, and Sam asks what he can get me to drink and I say *tea*, because I'm in White Out and that's what I always drink and then I **catch my breath**.

Then we just sit. Sam reaches across the table and takes my hand and we *just sit.*

Just sitting with someone you really, really like can be great, I've realized. I used to have this fear of "date silence". It made me talk the way my nine-year-old brother Max does with his friends – *ohne Punkt und Komma* type speech my dad calls it. Something like this: unddannhaterzuderMamagesagtdaskannstdunicht-machendasgehtnicht

Now I'm more **mature**. With Sam, I can just enjoy the fact that I'm sitting in a café in London with someone I really, really like. Great, eh?

It can't last. I said at the start that our weather forecast was *cloudy*, remember?

"Ed's got rugby practice tonight," Sam says nervously, "so I thought it was safe to come here. I know you like it."

I have the feeling that Sam's been planning his opening sentence for a while. It's a good tactic: start with the subject of Ed and get it out of the way. I sigh. I don't feel much like talking about Ed, but it's also clear something is **bothering** Sam.

I'm itching to take a couple of pictures, but it's clear

+++ to pant – keuchen +++ to catch one's breath – zu Atem kommen +++ mature – reif +++ to bother – *hier:* beschäftigen +++ I'm itching to ... – Es juckt mich ... +++

we have to talk first. I ask if Ed knows anything about us. Sam **shrugs his shoulders** and mumbles *no, no, no* but something *is* wrong. It's not always easy to get Sam to talk about difficult subjects. "Sam? What's up?" I say, in a voice I seem to have borrowed from Miss Bardwell.

And then I get the truth. Sam's still holding my hand and he's tapping his fingers gently on mine now. He's worried. "It's our website. Coffee on my trainers, remember?"

"Coffee on my trainers" was our sweet cyber-revenge for Ed's "Babe Blog". Maudie, Kim and me wrote it, my pictures were on it and Sam designed it. It was full of jokes about Ed and made him look like a **dork**. It was my favourite website of all time, ever, of course.

There's more. "Ed's so … ***suspicious***." Sam looks around, as though scared Ed is here now, dressed up as Mrs White or something. "He won't stop talking about the fact that none of you girls know much about computers, so you couldn't have done the website alone."

It's a sexist comment, obviously, but Ed's right, unfortunately. I don't know enough HTML to write my name, **never mind** create a website. There's more.

"Ed really wants to find out who designed the site. He was even talking about hiring a private detective at one point. He's totally paranoid. He told me he thought Steve might have done it the other day!!

"Steve!" I gasp. Steve's the lead singer of the Kitty

+++ to shrug one's shoulders – mit den Schultern zucken +++ dork – Depp +++ suspicious – misstrauisch +++ never mind – *hier:* geschweige denn +++

Gagarins and, well, a bit of a joker. (He thinks.) He's got the same nasty sense of humour as Ed, actually.

Sam sighs. "Yeah, Steve thought the site was really funny and kept making jokes. It's all really **spoiling** the atmosphere in the band at the moment. Nobody is looking forward to the recording session."

Sam takes off his glasses and looks me straight in the eyes. "Maybe I should just tell him it was me," he mumbles. "**Get it over with**." Sam has tired eyes.

I'm tired, too, actually. Tired of worrying about Ed. I just want his ghost out of things with Sam. I want him, what do they call it? *Exorcised*, that's it. I care about Sam enough to face Ed Stanton again. I suddenly realize what I have to do. Time to be Emily Hausmann, exorcist, **ghostbuster**!

"I'll talk to Ed," I say **boldly**. "I'll tell him that we got a professional designer to do our website. That'll be the end of it. Then you can all forget about it and make music and you don't have to worry." Easy.

Sam protests a bit. But only a little bit. I can tell that he *would* be **relieved** if I did talk to Ed.

Sam had already ordered us a pot of tea and – what else? – chips, and here comes Mrs White, co-owner of White Out, with them now. She **winks**, as usual, at us. Just as I think she's about to leave, she leans over and whispers to me, "Glad to see you **got rid of** the other boy, love. This one's a **wee** Scottish cracker!"

+++ to spoil – verderben +++ to get it over with – etwas hinter sich bringen +++ ghostbuster – Geisterauastreiber/in +++ bold – mutig +++ relieved – erleichtert +++ to wink – zwinkern +++ to get rid of s.o./sth. – jmdn./etwas los werden +++ wee – klein +++

Then she just squeezes Sam on the cheek! Like he's five or something! I can't help it, I say quickly, "Mrs White, would you mind if I took your picture?" and Mrs White **squeals** and **hugs** Sam and it's such a beautiful image, Mrs White hugging a terrified looking Sam, that I shoot the same scene about 20 times.

Mrs White disappears and Sam and me laugh for a moment about what happened. Our minds are really on more serious business, though, and soon **it's settled**. I will talk to Ed. I just have to think of a way to see him now. If I were to contact him directly, it would seem strange. He'd never even pick up the phone.

"The best thing," I say thoughtfully, squeezing some brown sauce, too much brown sauce, on my chips,

+++ to squeal – kreischen +++ to hug – umarmen +++ it's settled – es ist beschlossen +++

"would be to run into Ed somewhere, *accidentally*. You know, *Oh hi, Ed,* ***fancy seeing you here****? Did you know we hired a website designer? Yes, bye, see you.*"

Sam looks **uneasy** but he's thought of something, I'm sure. Then he smiles. "Actually, I can tell you *exactly* how to *run into* Ed Stanton between 7 and 8 pm on Thursday."

+++ Fancy seeing you here – Ach, du auch hier? +++ uneasy – unbehaglich +++

The Things We Do for Love

Sam **hesitates** and then says, "Ed has a little secret, you know. He's **addicted to** …" Sam pauses for effect and I gasp. Like a fool. "He's addicted to … chicken." Sam bursts out laughing. I look at him **blankly**.

"No, really," grins Sam. "He starts to get cold sweats if he doesn't eat at least a packet of it a day. And chicken **flavour** crisps – Ed can't get enough of them. His dorm *stinks*."

I shake my head. *Chicken*. Ed kept it well hidden. Most addicts are good at covering things up. They live a lie.

Sam's still smiling. "Anyway, Ed's *dealer* is *Supersavers*. You know, the supermarket? He always goes at seven o'clock on a Thursday night. It's *Supersupersaver Hour* then. 20% off everything for one hour only. The whole place is full of old people fighting to get to their favourite biscuits. It's *crazy*."

And so is Ed. He's rich – or rather his father is – but he's *sooooo* **mean** with his money. I can't believe that he shops during **discount** hour. Actually, I can. He was

+++ to hesitate – zögern +++ to be addicted to – abhängig sein von +++ blank – leer +++ flavour – Geschmack +++ mean – *hier:* geizig +++ discount – Rabatt +++

always "borrowing" money from his girlfriends. Charming, he was.

"You can't miss Ed at *Supersavers.* He'll be the only one under 80, carrying a basket full of chicken!"

"Right," I say, uncertainly. It's very real, suddenly – the prospect of meeting Ed Stanton again.

"I'll give you a kiss if you manage it," Sam whispers a bit shyly.

"Payment **in advance**," I say, cheekily, and Sam, shy Sam! just leans across the table and does indeed kiss me quite passionately. Mr White, former boxer, owner of the café, whistles from behind the **counter**. "Easy tiger!" he calls out.

Sam stops kissing and laughs. Then he looks at me **tenderly**. "Emily, when I said Ed was an addict, you didn't think I really meant …"

"Well, the rock 'n' roll lifestyle." I mutter. And then off I go, to finish off my films by taking more pictures of White Out, including some shots of Mr White standing proudly next to his boxing trophies. I try not to think about what a fool I am – chicken. Hmm.

And that, ladies and gentlemen, boys and girls, is how I came to find myself wandering around *Supersavers* supermarket, Camden, on Thursday evening. I feel like a mad stalker. I'm scared, in fact. Sam's the only one who knows about my mission. I'm meeting Maudie and Kim later but didn't **dare** tell them. They'd **freak out**!

+++ in advance – im Voraus +++ counter – Theke +++ tender – zärtlich ++++++ to dare – wagen +++ to freak out – ausflippen +++

Supersavers is huge, like most British supermarkets. Back in Berlin, we always used to go to lots of different shops – the *Bioladen*, the *Fleischer*, the **fishmongers**, the **stationers** – but in Britain everyone seems to drive in cars like **tanks** to one store the size of Nordrhein-Westfalen and buy everything there. I mean *everything* – I bet they have a **coffins** section here.

I arrive at *Supersavers* at 6.45. By 7, the place is starting to fill up, mainly with determined-looking pensioners. Sam's right – Ed and me will be the only ones here with our own teeth. Even so, I still haven't seen Ed. At the moment I haven't even found where the meat section is. You need a GPS system to navigate your way.

I'm lost. And suddenly this seems like a really stupid idea. I'm now in the "Biscuits and Cakes" section. It's full of old ladies filling their trolleys with the same

+++ fishmonger – Fischhändler +++ stationer – Schreibwarenhändler +++ tank – Panzer +++ coffin – Sarg +++

things that the Queen Mother likes – **ginger** biscuits, vanilla slices, Battenburg cake. Ooh! Jaffa Cakes – Soft Cakes we call them back home. Top. Jammie dodgers too – smiley face biscuits! Might as well get a few packs. Maybe *Supersupersaver Hour* is not so bad.

I have to hurry, though; it's now half past seven. Time's running out. *Concentrate. Stay on Ed's trail.* I see a sign saying: "Snacks and Soft Drinks." He might be getting his crisps. I take a few steps and *bingo!* there's Ed.

Or at least there's Ed's back. I'd know Ed anywhere, from any **angle** – he has the body of a rugby player and the long blond hair of a wannabe rockstar. Unmistake-able.

My heart is in my mouth. I don't want to jump him – Boo! – and calling out seems stupid too: *Oh Edvard! It's me, Emily, ze German girl* I decide that the best thing to do is to double back down the **aisle** I've been in. It'll be easier if we walk towards each other. More natural. Yeah. Totally natural, this whole scene.

It works though, and here we finally stand: *Ed Stanton v Emily Hausmann. Face to face.* Or, actually, shopping basket to shopping basket. It's a very confusing feeling. I haven't seen Ed since our last date, the day of the Kitty Gagarins' photo shoot. We kissed then. For half a moment, I can't help it. I remember how it was to kiss Ed Stanton. My shopping basket starts to shake a little.

This is just a **guess**, but I don't think Ed is remember-

+++ ginger – Ingwer +++ angle – Winkel +++ My heart is in my mouth – Das Herz schlägt mir bis zum Hals +++ aisle – Gang +++ guess – Vermutung +++

ing the last time we kissed. He does look a bit shaky, too, though. He's reaching for a bag of crisps the same size as my nine-year-old brother Max (and he's big for his age) when he sees me. Ed takes his hand away and his mouth falls open, as if he's just been told that he's got six days to live or something. *Emily the Exorcist, his worst nightmare.*

Both Ed and me are now just staring very, very hard at each others' shopping baskets. I'm fascinated by Ed's, if I'm honest. Sam wasn't joking. Ed's basket already has about 15 packets of cooked chicken in it. What a *freak*.

I'm suddenly a bit embarrassed by all the cakes and biscuits in my basket. I hope Ed doesn't think I'm trying to heal my broken heart by comfort eating. Luckily, he seems more interested in trying to decide whether or not I've followed him here tonight.

"Haven't seen you in here before," he mutters. Ed's eyes meet mine, finally, and my heart – *Verräter*! – gives a jump. He nods in the direction of my shopping basket. "Having a children's birthday party, are you?"

I blush. I'm trying to channel some of Auntie Nora's energy right now. She's always really cool in these situations. I smile and shrug my shoulders. "No, just having a few friends over to the common room later. Maudie, Kim – remember them?" Then I nod towards *his* basket. "You're opening your own KFC franchise, right?"

Now it's Ed's turn to go red. He must hate me. He's had enough: he wants to get away from me already, I can tell. His eyes are looking towards the cash desks and the exits behind my head.

And then a little chicken-flavoured miracle happens – Ed's face changes. It's as though he's realized this is his chance to ask *me* a couple of things, too.

"By the way, *congratulations*." His voice is as cold as the chicken in his basket. "*Great* website. I didn't realize that you were such a computer genius. Bill Gates been on the phone offering you a job yet?"

It's my big moment and I'm not going to mess it up. "I didn't do the website," I say, simply. "I hired someone from an agency to do it for us."

Ed's eyebrows lower for a second, shadowing his eyes. Then he **scrunches up** his nose, suspiciously. He's still not quite sure: "I didn't think you'd have enough money," he sniffs. Man, he really is a snob.

"Oh, that was no problem," I say a bit too loudly. "There were ***plenty* of** girls who wanted to pay something." An **elderly** woman pushing a trolley completely full of cat food stares at us nervously and tries to walk faster.

Ed **flicks** his long, blond Goldilocks hair. It always hangs over his eyes. It's actually a miracle he found anything here tonight. Now he's convinced, I know it. "Whatever," he mutters.

It's over. Ed and me both make the same kind of **caveman** sound at each other – *ugghtze.* A sound that means something like, I **sort of** hate you but goodbye anyway. *Ugghtze.* And Ed's gone. Again.

+++ to scrunch up – (Nase) rümpfen +++ plenty of – viele +++ elderly – älter +++ to flick – *hier:* zurückwerfen +++ caveman – Höhlenmensch +++ sort of – irgendwie +++

The Independent Republic of Bloomsbury

Mission – possible! I text Sam on my way back to school: *Operation Chicken Run Successful!* I can hardly push the buttons on my phone because of all the shopping I'm carrying. Although I was only supposed to be "accidentally" running into Ed, I've bought two bags of **treats**! I've spent 26 pounds and 57 pence! *Weil ich es mir wert bin.* I deserve it.

Maudie and Kim are both coming over to the Kensington common room tonight. It will be their first time in the "ghetto". I want them to see how I have to suffer, how bad Kensington House really is. I'm even hoping that I'll be able to introduce them to Amanda. I have a nasty feeling I talk about her all the time. Maybe now the girls will actually understand why.

I carry the bags of food up to the common room. There are only two girls there – playing **chess**. It's perfect. In the Bloomsbury common room right now, they're probably listening to Drum 'n' Bass and digging tunnels under the road to St Dougan's to see boys. It's *another planet.*

At eight, Maudie and Kim arrive. They're both in

+++ treat – Leckerei +++ chess – Schach +++

their uniforms, which is unusual. Normally they change out of them as soon as lessons are over but tonight, they tell me, they had an "extra study meeting" and they didn't have time.

When I say she's "wearing a uniform" Maudie, in fact, seems to be "wearing what they call uniform in Bloomsbury". She's got a lot of black eyeliner on as usual (illegal) as well as a pair of bright yellow leggings! (Even more illegal.)

The Chalk Farm school colours are actually burgundy and yellow – a dream combination, **fashionistas**! – but we must *only* wear burgundy **tights**, bought from Broughton's, the uniform shop. They're awful. They *itch.* It's like wearing a mosquitoe nest on your legs.

Maudie's leggings not only look nice and soft: they actually look really good. Burgundy skirt with burgundy tights and burgundy and yellow tie = totally boring. Burgundy tights with burgundy and yellow tie and bright yellow leggings = radical. A little bit Emo.

"Wow," I say, trying not to sound jealous. "Those are *cool* leggings."

Maudie grins. "You like them? School colours. Mrs McKee agreed."

Mrs McKee is the Bloomsbury housemistress. She *agreed.* Just like that. As if Maudie had asked to go to the toilet or something. I want to cry.

Maudie doesn't even notice my inner pain. "Mrs McKee said she liked the fact I was playing with the *school aesthetic* … Ooh!"

+++ fashionista – Modefan +++ tights – Strumpfhose +++

Maudie's just spotted the packets of biscuits I've laid out. Kim squeals, too, when she sees them. "Jaffa cakes! **Yummy**!" She laughs. "Quite a lot of food, Emily. Do you have to **gain weight** for a film role or something? Playing a sumo are you?"

"I had to do a bit of shopping," I say, simply. "And, after surviving meeting he-who-must-not-be named, I thought I deserved some treats."

Ed really is a bit like Lord Voldemort: you know, evil, has a lot of fans, the three of us never talk about him anymore. You know. *I* thought it was funny. Harry Potter jokes at boarding school – *you* try and not make them.

The girls are shocked. Kim actually drops the biscuit in her hand, as if it were covered in Ed Stanton and/or

+++ yummy – lecker +++ to gain weight – zunehmen +++

anthrax. I tell the girls everything; all about Sam and the **tension** in the band and how I wanted to help.

When I've finished, Maudie and Kim are silent for a moment. Then, as though now satisfied that her biscuit had no physical contact with Ed Stanton, Kim reaches for it again.

"Emily, you're a star," she says, **munching** her Jammie Dodger. "You're like a … **warrior** princess or something. I couldn't have done it." She **shivers.**

I protest, of course – *it was nothing!* – but secretly I *am* proud that I faced Ed.

It's Maudie's turn now. She's working her way through the biscuits, too, but finds time to say, "And Sam's worth it, he really is. We both think he's *great.*"

She looks thoughtful. "Actually, we wondered if you wanted to bring him with you to the Bloomsbury Christmas party. We're allowed to invite two guests each."

I'm halfway through a Jammie Dodger myself now and it nearly gets stuck in my throat. "*Whaaat?*" I **splutter, crumbs** flying everywhere. Sam's, well, a *boy.* A boy here in our *all girls* school? Like, *hello??*

"**Check!**," says one of the girls playing chess, looking over **in disgust**. I suddenly notice that the area where we've been sitting is covered in biscuit crumbs. Oh, I'll clear it up later! This is important!

+++ anthrax – Anthrax (Substanz, die Milzbrand verursacht) +++ tension – Spannung +++ to munch – mampfen +++ warrior – Krieger/in +++ to shiver – frösteln +++ to splutter – hervorstoßen +++ crumb – Krümel +++ Check! – Schach! +++ in disgust – angeekelt +++

"You do know that no boys are allowed in our school, right?" I gasp.

It's true. I even know the number of the School Rule. Number 54. *Boys are not permitted on the* ***premises*** *of Chalk Farm School for Girls without the agreement of the Housemistress.* It broke my heart when I read it. And I still remember that there was nearly a ***riot*** when a boy – Ed Stanton – was allowed to speak at one of our assemblies.

"Yeah," says Maudie, casually. "But we *do* have the permission of our Housemistress. Mrs McKee's totally fine with it."

If I were any older than 14, I'd probably have a heart attack. I repeat, dumbly: "You're allowed to have a party with boys at it?" I think I've lost all the feeling in my legs. And my arms. And my brain.

Kim smiles. "We told you Mrs McKee was cool." She says this while reading the back of the packet of Jammie Dodgers. "Do you both know how many grammes of fat there are in one of these? It's like all the fat you should eat, ever, in the whole of your life."

Kim does a lot of ballet and has probably doubled her own body weight by eating one little biscuit. But I'm not interested in grammes of fat. I'm interested in **proper** parties that have boys at them!

"Miss Bardwell tries to stop our party every year. She hates it but there's *nothing* she can do," says Maudie proudly. "We're the independent republic of Blooms-

+++ premises – Gelände +++ riot – Aufstand +++ proper – richtig +++

bury. And guess who's the DJ this year? Me!" She looks really pleased; she's mad about music, Maudie.

"One day Miss Bardwell will get some tanks and guns together and invade you," I joke. I can really see Miss Bardwell, wind blowing through her hair, off on her mission to protect innocent girls from the evils of having *fun.*

Maudie is warming to her subject now, really excited. "Sorry, Emily, but your party is always ***lame.*** The only boys at yours will be a couple of Dads and *Santa. Santa's* always Mr Michaels dressed up by the way."

"Oh no!" I groan. Mr Michaels is Miss Bardwell's boyfriend. They've been together for eleven years. You get less for **murder**.

"But at Bloomsbury we have a *Secret Santa,* where we all buy each other something, so you get really nice stuff – accessories, toiletries, DVDs."

Kim and Maudie try to remember what fantastic, cool, amazing thing they got in the Bloomsbury *Secret Santa* last year, but I don't hear them. My ears are too full of bitterness. I knew that first day at Chalk Farm School that I should have listened to my heart – and to Nora. I should really have been a "warrior princess" and just told Miss Bardwell: *I'll be going to Bloomsbury and not Kensington, thanks very much.* Then I wouldn't be suffering as I am now. Still, at least I've got Maudie and Kim. And my golden ticket for Sam and me to the party of the year!

Then the room temperature drops suddenly. The air

+++ lame – lahm +++ murder – Mord +++

feels damp and cold. Round my throat – a tight **sensation**. I hear a laugh that sounds **familiar**. I look up, and my blood turns to ice. Standing behind Kasparov and Fisher in the corner and listening to every word is – Cyclops.

She's alone. This is unusual as, like most divas, Amanda *always* seems to travel with an **entourage**. She's looking over at Kim and Maudie with interest. What's she up to?

"Ladies!" she cries warmly. "What are you cool chicks doing over here in Loserville?"

When I was trying to **convince** myself that having Amanda in the dorm might be better than having Olga, I actually made a list. Olga **versus** Amanda. I wrote down things like: *Olga – You can never work out what she'll do, or why. Amanda – She's transparent. You always know what she's up to.*

I can see through her right now. She's practically **rubbing** herself **against** Maudie and Kim. Compliment follows compliment: Kim "has an amazing figure, great **posture**" and Maudie's "hair is soooo shiny? Caviar **rinse**?"

Then Amanda just comes out and says it. No messing around: "So it's nearly Christmas time, girls, eh? Party season. I suppose ours will be deadly boring as usual. Chosen your two guests yet?" She's fishing for a ticket to the Bloomsbury party. Clear as day.

+++ sensation – Gefühl +++ familiar – bekannt +++ entourage – Gefolge +++ to convince – überzeugen +++ versus – gegen +++ to rub oneself against – sich an jmdm. reiben, heranschmeißen +++ posture – Haltung +++ rinse – Spülung +++

Kim looks at Maudie. Maudie looks at me. I look at Kim. Maudie looks at Kim. Amanda looks at Kim. Kim looks at the packet of Jammie Dodgers.

Then Kim says slowly, uncertainly, "Yeahhh, we've got our guests."

"Emily, of course," says Maudie quickly, loyally. "And Emily's b…"

Nooooo! Stoooopppppp!!! Maudie's about to say "boyfriend" and I don't want Amanda to find out about Sam. The less she knows the better: knowledge is power.

"b…een really looking forward to it," I interrupt a bit breathlessly. Maudie gives me a funny look.

Amanda's suspicious. And **disappointed**. She smiles though, ever the Charm School Princess, and says lightly, "Oh well, Emily, *of course*. So important for her to see a bit of our culture before she finally goes home to Germany *forever*."

I open my mouth to say something, then close it again. Life's too short.

Amanda goes on, optimistically: "If you *do* hear of anyone who's got an invitation, I'd love to come over to Bloomsbury. You guys are so cool. Such a great atmosphere in your house. So alternative. **Bohemian**."

Pah! Amanda's about as "alternative" and "bohemian" as my Onkel Dieter's *Schlager* collection. I've heard enough. Life's not *that* short.

"But Amanda," I say **cattily**, "the party's on a *Saturday* night. You couldn't miss the *Windswept Love Christ-*

+++ disappointed – enttäuscht +++ bohemian – unkonventionell +++ catty – gehässig +++

mas Special. All the animals getting their presents. Oh, their little faces!"

Amanda colours. It's the colour of shame, I'm happy to see. Being a huge *Windswept Love fan* is, *natürlich*, not very bohemian. Ha! She **glares at** me, then murmurs something about having to "rest her eye".

Kim makes a sympathetic face. "Does it hurt a lot?"

"Oh, you know, just *all the time* …" Amanda looks depressed.

Maudie **clucks**. It's a noise that says: *Poor Amanda!*

Between you and me, this meeting with Amanda isn't going quite as I'd imagined. Cyclops hasn't got Maudie and Kim to invite her to the party. But I'd thought that Maudie and Kim would *hate* Amanda instinctively and, it's clear, they don't. I'm realising that when Amanda wants to get someone to like her – or *needs* to get someone to like her – then she's actually pretty good at it. Take Miss Bardwell. Amanda obviously decided to **charm** her and it totally worked.

And now look at her. She's going through some old ballet moves she "learned as a kid" with Kim. She's a good mover, Amanda, **graceful**. Kim's **impressed**, I can see. She's even telling Amanda that she's going to apply to dance college. I didn't know that! Suddenly I feel a bit *graceless*.

Amanda's revealing to the girls that she's off to Thailand for Christmas. I didn't know that either. Oh God, this is awful: they're all ***bonding***! They're totally opening

+++ to glare at s.o. – jmdn. zornig anstarren +++ to cluck – mit der Zunge schnalzen +++ to charm – bezaubern +++ graceful – anmutig +++ impressed – beeindruckt +++ to bond – sich verbünden +++

their hearts to each other! Thank goodness Cyclops is finally leaving before they can all get matching tattoos or something.

"See you around," she smiles in a friendly, easy way. She's even pleasant to me: *Catch you later, Emily!*

No one says anything for a moment after she goes. This meeting's been a public relations disaster for me, **frankly**. I have the feeling that Kim and Maudie really thought Amanda was *OK*. I have to ask.

"So, you finally got to meet Cyclops!" I sound uneasy.

Kim **winces**. "Do you have to call her that? Not really cool to make fun of her eye, is it? I probably wouldn't want to share a room with her or anything but …"

No, you wouldn't, I think, darkly. Kim has a double room, which she shares with Clarissa Dunn, one of the nicest, kindest, sweetest girls in the world, apparently. Kim has *no idea.*

"Amanda's not quite the monster I'd imagined, to be honest," says Maudie quietly.

Nightmare. Amanda has successfully made me look like a **twisted sister** in front of my new friends. Maudie and Kim are too nice, that's the problem. No functioning *Zickenradar*. The fools.

They're leaving me, too, now. They've had enough of me. I take a last look at Maudie's leggings as she goes through the common room door. *Great* leggings. I think I'll get myself a pair next time I'm up Camden High Street. School colours, right?

+++ frankly – offen gesagt +++ to wince – zusammenzucken +++ twisted sister – überspannte Tussi +++

Vorfreude, schönste Freude

1:0 to Amanda. But I have the feeling there will be plenty more fun and games with her so I'm not too depressed. Anyway, all this Christmas party talk has got me thinking AGAIN about the big question – Berlin or England for the holidays?

I go to check my e-mails. My parents must have decided what they're doing by now. And, finally, they have. There's a mail from my Dad: *Betreff: Weihnachten!* There's also a very interesting sounding mail from my friend Merle: *Betreff: Bettis elvischer Stalker* – but I'm a good girl and read Dad's first:

Töchterlein! Wie geht's dir?? Es ist offensichtlich total wichtig, dieses Jahr bei Ihrer Majestät zu sein. Das heißt – wir kommen nach England! Flüge wurden heute gebucht – 23. Dezember. Ist dir das recht? Ich muss am 2. Januar wieder in Berlin sein – wir können also leider nicht die Schule besuchen. Es gibt auch Gerüchte, dass deine Tante Nora im Lande sein wird. Bei euch gibt es doch sicherlich auch ein Feuerwerk, oder?!

Fireworks. Hmmm. Great outdoors at Silvester, not so great indoors at Christmas. I say a silent prayer: *Please, don't let the Queen Mother and my dad fight as much as they normally do. And please let Nora be there. But please don't let her fight as much as she normally does with the Queen Mother. Thanks.*

I read Merle's mail next. She asks what I'm doing at Christmas, of course, and at least now I can tell her. I feel pretty sad that I won't see Betti und Merle but they are now certain they'll have saved enough money by spring to visit London. *Wir haben jetzt fast 100 Euro in unserem Sparfond! Das reicht wahrscheinlich doch für Ryanair oder??*

Otherwise, Merle's mail is full of the usual school **gossip** from Hermann-Hesse: Betti is still being romanced in Elvish – and scared to death probably – by Lars-Christoph Schmid, the Gothic *Herr der Ringe* fan. *Superzicke* Katharina Müller is still going out with gorgeous Andreas Kutschke and can't stop **showing off** about it. And Sebastian Junger, my old **crush**, is a bit low: … *und er hat wieder gefragt, wie er am besten mit dir in Kontakt treten soll, macht aber nichts, oder?*

I answer Merle, letting her know about Christmas and a *bit* about Sam, too, of course. Nothing like those stupid childish e-mails I wrote when I was dating Ed, though. Back then, I told Betti and Merle that Ed was "the one" and **stuff** – *peinlich.* I'm playing it cool this time. I'm totally philosophical: *Sam ist ein super Typ. Mal sehen, was aus uns wird.* I've learned my lesson.

Then I check out what some of the other people from

+++ otherwise – ansonsten +++ gossip – Klatsch und Tratsch +++ to show off – angeben +++ crush – *hier:* Flamme, Liebelei +++ stuff – Zeug +++

my class are doing in their entries on SchülerVZ. I never look to see what Katharina Müller is up to: *Mein Traumleben mit dem Traumprinzen* probably. And I never look Sebastian Junger up either. What is he playing at by the way? He has both my phone number and my e-mail address. He could have made contact any time. But now, of course, I'm secretly glad that he hasn't.

To bed. Luckily, Amanda also seems tired tonight and she's actually asleep not long after lights out. Unlike me: I can't stop thinking about Christmas. My parents and brother will miss the Kensington party. It will also be too late for them to look around the school and chat to Miss Bardwell. Brilliant!

Sam will have gone to Scotland too by then, I suppose. Thank goodness again. I try to imagine him meeting my dad, who would just make bad jokes and do his "comedy German"/Onkel-Dieter act: *Do zhou vont to marry my daughter?* I'd rather eat my own feet than sit through that. I'm totally proud of Sam and showing him off to Betti and Merle would be a very different thing. But Sam + my family = death from **shame**.

I'm just sort of drifting off to sleep – I'm a bit scared that I've been thinking of Onkel Dieter so much today that I'll dream about him – when I notice Melissa. She's in bed and even though the lights are out, I can see that her eyes are open. Open and *very* bright and shiny. Has she been crying? How would I know? When was the last time I had a proper chat with Melissa? She's had a terri-

+++ shame – Scham +++

ble time **recently** and we haven't once discussed how she's feeling. Hmmmm.

Melissa Kerr. I really like her, actually. She's always been kind to me. When I first met her, on Day One here, she was a happy, simple soul who loved three things: her horse, my fellow *Landsmann* Almonds; her brother Josh, rugby star of St Dougan's; and Olga Petrova, **enigmatic** holder of both Russian and American passports. Really, you had the feeling that as long as those three people/animals were in Melissa's life, things were perfect.

Then Josh and Olga got together and it was ***Das vidanya*** to Melissa's beautiful Anglo-Russian alliance with Olga. Olga lied to Melissa about dating her brother and ended up moving out of our dorm. Melissa's now "officially" friends with Becks, but swapping Olga for Becks is rather like swapping a beautiful, **pedigree** poodle for a big, muddy, noisy Labrador. I know from Becks that Melissa is talking again to Josh but 1) not very often, 2) they *absolutely never* discuss Olga.

She has been really quiet lately, Melissa. Really **flat**. It would be great to try and cheer her up a bit. Then it comes to me, in a shower of **tinsel** and fairy dust. The party! The Bloomsbury Christmas party! Everyone who's anyone is talking about it! Everyone who's anyone wants to go! There's even a black market for tickets – I heard a rumour that one rich girl in Knightsbridge offered a Bloomsbury girl *50 pounds* to invite her!

+++ recently – in letzter Zeit +++ enigmatic – rätselhaft +++ Das vidanya (russisch) – Auf Wiedersehen +++ pedigree – Rassehund +++ flat – matt +++ tinsel – Flitter +++

I'll get Maudie and Kim to invite Melissa to a party with real live BOYS at it. If that doesn't put a smile on Melissa's face, *nothing* will.

I'd love to say that, after deciding how to help Melissa, I then fell into a deep peaceful sleep. But I didn't. I fell into a restless, uneasy sleep, having nightmares about being lost in the *Spreewald* on a moped with Onkel Dieter, just like *I knew I would.*

Friday night: I'm meeting Sam at "The Odeon", a small art house cinema near our schools. It's 6.30 pm as I walk down Camden High Street to get there. There's still a lot going on – there's always a lot going on in Camden – though some of the shops are already closed.

My wandering eye stops at a shop that is still open. It's one that's quite popular with the girls at Chalk Farm and which sells **jewellery** and bags and – ooh, hello! – *tights. Leggings.* I'm pretty sure that Maudie got her cool yellow ones here. You know what? I'm not running *that* late for Sam – I'll have a quick look inside.

Nine minutes later I am the proud owner of one pair of bright yellow leggings! Just like Maudie's! I'll probably never wear them but even just *having* them is somehow exciting. That's how *boring* my life is.

Not that boring – it's Sam time again. That's always *fascinating.* We meet in the foyer, get our tickets, a *super super size me* popcorn to share. (Dinner was beef olives tonight, OK? Honestly, no wonder so many British people are vegetarian.) Then we settle down in our seats,

+++ jewellery – Schmuck +++

deep and comfortable, and stare up at The Odeon's lovely **wedding** cake **ceilings**.

The cinema's beautiful, built in the 1920s. It's half empty, too – perfect conditions for marrying together some lips. Woo hoo!!!

Sam chose the film we're "seeing", an old Japanese one, and we talk a bit before it starts – I can't wait two hours to hear how things are with Ed. The news is good: "It's all much better," grins Sam. "Ed told us that he 'found out' that you paid someone to design the website. He was so relieved and everyone in the band is much more relaxed again. Thanks, Emily, that was a really cool thing to do."

I'm a regular Father Christmas right now, don't you think? **Spreading** love, peace and happiness wherever I go. It feels good. Speaking of Christmas: I **mention** the Bloomsbury Christmas party to Sam – he's enthusiastic. The Bloomsbury Party is even a legend at St Dougan's, it seems. Strangely enough, a lot of the boys there are also interested in being invited over for an evening at an all-girls school: "Guys kill to go to that party. I'm *not* joking."

Sam looks thoughtful for a moment. We're now half watching the adverts. "I'm leaving for Scotland the day after the party." It's dark but I think Sam's blushing a bit. "We haven't talked about the Christmas holidays, have we? I was pretty sure you'd be going back to Berlin."

He looks disappointed when I tell him that I'm actu-

+++ wedding – Hochzeit +++ ceiling – Decke +++ to spread – verteilen +++ to mention – erwähnen +++

ally staying in Britain. "You could have come with me to Edinburgh for Hogmanay. You know, the Scottish New Year? They have an amazing street party there. Or I could have stuck around here a bit longer. But Mum wants me back home. Things are …"

Sam's really whispering now; I can hardly hear him. He doesn't finish his sentence. I realise that I know very little about him. I try to remember what information I have about Sam's home life. My brain opens the memory file called "Sam Reid". It's not exactly 12 gb big or anything:

Has brothers, lots (2 or 3???). One is called "Cameron". (Made me think of Cameron Diaz.) Parents divorced. Lives with his mum when he's home (near Glasgow, can't remember the town, funny name). Parents still friendly – his dad lives nearby. Supports one of the big football teams in Glasgow. Can't remember which one. Plays drums. Loves computers. Bites fingernails. ***Generous.*** *Funny. Good friends with Matt, bass player in KGs. Great kisser. Seems to like me.*

That's really *everything* I know about Sam Reid. He might have all kinds of funny meat addictions or secret websites on the Internet. I wonder quickly whether or not I should Google him, just to be sure.

Sam Reid puts his arm round my shoulder. The feeling that I get – shivery and warm and safe and scared – seems to **erase** my memory. I totally forget to ask him

+++ generous – großzügig +++ to erase – auslöschen +++

what he was going to say. *Things at home are* … what exactly?? The film is starting anyway.

I put my hand on Sam's knee. Then Sam starts to kiss me again … pardon? The film, you ask? Oh, it's the moving and beautiful story of some Japanese people who have died and want to go to heaven. Before they can do this, they have to choose one memory from their life – their favourite moment – to take with them.

At least that's what I read in the foyer. To be honest, there's too much top kissing action with Sam for me to really follow the story. It's not a total waste of money (ten pounds each! 1.856 yen!) as the sound of an exotic language in the background makes everything seem even more romantic. All that Japanese. Mmmm.

Then, disappointingly, the lights go up. It's time to leave. Sam looks worried. "You know, we're in the studio on Thursday all day. The school actually gave us time off! We have to rehearse like crazy till then. What about a nice walk round Regent's Park in the freezing cold next Saturday?"

"Sounds cool," I grin. Then I wish Sam luck with the session. I *kiss* him luck with the session. Lovely kissing. How ever did I live without it before?

A Change Is as Good as a Rest

Back to life, back to reality. Reality. No dates for a week-type-reality. Just a **deadly** boring school life, in the world's worst school uniform …

Before I came here, I hated the idea of school uniform. My mum tried to convince me that it wasn't a totally bad thing, but the reality of life in uniform is that there are good and bad things about having to wear it. The good thing is you always wear the same thing every day – it's *easy*. The bad thing is you always wear the same thing every day – it's *boring*.

Then one morning, as I'm getting dressed, I remember a phrase that I learned from the Queen Mother: *a change is as good as a rest.* I look at my school uniform, laid out on my bed as usual. And I suddenly decide I will *die* if I have to wear the same thing again today. *Just do it.* I decide I'm bored enough to risk wearing my yellow leggings. A change! Nearly a rest!

"Oooh," say Melissa and Becks when they see my leggings. "You're brave!" Amanda just stares knowingly at me. Like she just *knows* I'm on a Kamikaze mission. Maybe I am.

+++ rest – *hier:* Pause +++ deadly – tödlich +++

But I'm a careful Kamikaze at least: I've picked the best day of the week to have 1968 legs. We won't see Miss Bardwell today. She has to go to some boring-sounding workshop for Latin teachers this morning. Miss Shaw, our lovely art teacher, will take **registration**. She won't mind a bit of sunshine yellow.

But Miss Shaw isn't taking registration today. Instead it's Mr Benn. He has some **fairly** awful news for us: Miss Shaw was knocked off her bike by a car yesterday on the way home from school. We're all shocked – everyone likes Miss Shaw. She'll be fine, Mr Benn tells us: "But she's broken her arm and is pretty **shaken**. She'll be **off sick** for the rest of the year. A **supply** teacher will take her place. He's arriving this morning."

He. A *man*! It's a magical word here. There aren't many male teachers at Chalk Farm School – the danger money isn't high enough, probably.

"Maybe he'll be some gorgeous, blond!" says Becks, **eagerly** and a bit too loudly. We all laugh. Mr Benn goes red, quickly checks our names and disappears. Like I said – he probably isn't paid enough for this. And he didn't notice my legs!

In fact, all day, I get zero negative feedback from our teachers and about 15 pieces of positive feedback on my leggings from other girls. Perhaps Kensington's a bit cooler than I thought. I relax. I'm actually quite looking forward to seeing our new Art teacher. Maybe Becks is right.

+++ registration – Anwesenheitsliste +++ fairly – ziemlich +++ shaken – durchgerüttelt +++ to be off sick – krank geschrieben sein +++ supply – *hier:* Ersatz +++ eager – eifrig +++

Becks *is* right, as it **turns out**. And horribly wrong. When we walk into our art class that afternoon, there is no Adonis waiting for us. Instead it's Medusa. Miss Bardwell is sitting there. She must have sharpened her face: it looks even more **pointed**. What's *she* doing here?

"Hello, girls!" she **booms**. "Surprise! I'm always free on Friday afternoons so I've decided that I shall teach my favourite group a bit of art. It will make a change from Latin! And you know what they say, *a change is as good as a rest*."

She's now telling us that she will not be teaching the nasty kind of get-your-clothes-dirty-and-express-yourself kind of art. No, no, no, no, no! Miss Bardwell will be teaching History of Art. Today's class will be on Van Gogh. We are to take notes. She will ask questions at the end. And she's **off** … *sunflowers* … ***starry*** *night* … *blah* … *cut ear* … *blah* …

I can't listen, I'm too *sad*. And I'm worried about another problem: I'm **dying to** get into the **darkroom**. I still have those films from White Out, remember? I haven't yet seen those classic scenes of Sam being crushed by Mrs White! (One might make a great Christmas present for him, now I think about it. Funny.) I can see the darkroom key now, hanging next to the blackboard. It's calling me: *Come to me, Emily!*

I try to think positively. Miss Bardwell might just let me have it, too, if I play my cards right. So I try to listen

+++ to turn out – sich herausstellen +++ pointed – spitz +++ to boom – dröhnen +++ to be off – *hier:* loslegen +++ starry – sternenklar +++ to be dying to do sth. – es kaum erwarten können, etwas zu tun +++ darkroom – Dunkelkammer +++

in class. I even answer a question! And at the end of the lesson, I put on my biggest, sweetest, **fakest** smile and go up to Miss Bardwell's desk.

But as she sees me coming towards her, Miss Bardwell is not checking out my cute smile. She's looking at my legs – my legg*ings*. I'd totally forgotten. I'm dead meat. The Taliban have a more relaxed dress code than Miss Bardwell. There's no hiding now.

I get my punishment quickly and at least it's not a public **stoning**. It is a real **drag**: now I've an *extra essay to write on Van Gogh's use of sunshine yellow. And if Miss Bardwell ever sees me in those leggings again she'll … oooh!* She can't even finish her sentence. She'll **strangle** me with them probably.

There was no point, of course, in even asking about the darkroom. I'm locked out.

My **mood** is as dark as the darkroom I now can't enter. The thought of not being able to develop my photos + not painting anything till *next year* + another hour and a half a week of Miss Bardwell for "Art": it's **unbearable**. To top it all, the supply teacher really is, I've heard, young and good-looking. *Every* group except ours has him.

I try to call Sam to cry a bit on his phone-shoulder but I get a strange message saying the number is **unavailable**. Perhaps Miss Bardwell is blocking all my calls? Maybe she's paid a **hitman** to get Sam?

+++ fake – falsch +++ stoning – Steinigung +++ drag – Langweiler +++ to strangle – erwürgen +++ mood – Laune +++ unbearable – unerträglich +++ unavailable – nicht erreichbar +++ hitman – Auftragskiller +++

No. There's a more boring reason, it seems. Sam calls me the next day – his mobile is "broken" and he's talking to me from the phone box at St Dougan's. We both agree we have **loads** to tell each other.

Saturday **dawns**, date day and it's a horrible one – it really is freezing cold. I make my way slowly to the place where we'd arranged to meet, at Clarence Bridge, near the boating lake in Regent's Park. Sam's already there, of course, standing on the bridge and throwing stones in the water.

I watch him for a moment. It's not *really* **spying**, I'm just coming up to one side of him and he hasn't seen me yet. Sam's dressed for the cold, in a big red and black **lumberjack** style jacket. He looks gorgeous, but he's absolutely *furious* about something.

I wonder what on earth is wrong. Sam's always so calm and gentle. Maybe it's Ed or the band. Or – oh no! Déjà vu! – maybe it's *me*. Something's just generally wrong with *me*.

I feel a bit **guilty**, staring at him secretly like this, so I call out loudly, "Hi!" Sam turns and his face changes at once. It **brightens**, softens. It doesn't really seem as if he's angry at me. We kiss a bit and that's bright and soft, too, and then we walk through the park a bit, holding hands. Sam talks a lot about how the recording session was, how nervous all the band were: "Even Ed, though he kept saying he wasn't!" They had a great engineer and …

+++ loads – jede Menge +++ to dawn – *hier:* beginnen +++ to spy – spionieren +++ lumberjack – Holzfäller +++ guilty – schuldbewusst +++ to brighten – aufhellen +++

I'm smiling and listening, truly. I've nearly stopped worrying, too. Perhaps Sam was just **annoyed** about school or something else before I arrived. That's probably it. Yes, probably.

"Ta Dah!" Sam's **beaming** at me proudly and holding out a CD: *Kitty Gagarins, first demo.* "Here it is! This will be worth millions on ebay one day! We do sound pretty hot, if I say so myself."

I want to hear it right now, of course. Sam's also got the track as a download on his iPod so we sit on a bench and share a pair of headphones and listen: *I don't like your rules and we're too cool for school*! It's a strange experience to hear the song in this way. Sitting on a bench in Regent's Park, with Sam's arm around my shoulder. And I'm hearing the band in a whole new other way, too. They don't just sound good, like they did

+++ annoyed – verärgert +++ to beam – strahlen +++

at the concert: they sound *amazing*. Professional. Steve's voice is deeper, more mature and … oh, it's brilliant!

I give Sam a hug and tell him everything I've been thinking. He's pleased and he's so **jolly** now, I'm almost certain that I really *was* imagining things before. We decide to go and get some lunch. Sam leads me to a beautiful place called the Garden Café. It's next to a rose garden, with an open-air theatre nearby. It's the kind of place you could imagine *Aschenputtel* **dropping in** to have a bite to eat with her prince in – it couldn't be any more romantic. We order some smoked Scottish **salmon** – "We have to!" jokes Sam – just as a starter.

Then Sam goes a bit quiet again. He keeps opening the menu, staring at it really hard and making strange faces. "I'm not that hungry," he says finally. "I think that's all I'm going to have. Just a starter and, emmm, a **tap** water."

"Oh, right," I mumble, "me, umm, too. Great." I'm actually *totally* hungry, but it seems a bit **greedy** to eat any more than Sam. He's much bigger than me.

So we **nibble** on our salmon and sip our tap waters and Sam tells me about how he used to go fishing with his grandfather. Everything is fine, nice even, until I ask about Sam's phone and then – suddenly! – storm warning! Sam's face darkens again. "It's really broken," he says slowly. "It's annoying but … I'm getting a new one for Christmas. I can still call you from the payphone. **No big deal**."

+++ jolly – gut gelaunt +++ to drop in – vorbeischauen +++ salmon – Lachs +++ tap – Wasserhahn +++ greedy – gierig, gefräßig +++ to nibble – knabbern +++ No big deal – Kein Problem +++

I'll tell you what *is* a big deal, ladies – trust. It's a **fragile** thing, too. I can't quite put my finger on it right now. It's not that I think Sam is *lying* to me about his phone, it's just that I have a funny feeling that something is not quite true. Call it female intuition. Call it paranoia. Call it, oh, call it whatever you like! The thing with the phone is *strange*, OK?

At four o'clock Sam looks at his watch and says, "Let's get the **bill**. I've really got to get back. I need to call my mum. From the phone box, obviously. Lucky thing I'm the only boy in London without a mobile. It's like my private line."

Call his mum? I suddenly feel a bit sick. This can't be happening again, can it? It would be like being hit by relationship **lightning**. Being dumped after three dates by two guys within two months?

We end up splitting the bill. Sam tries to pay it, but when I offer my half, he looks a bit relieved, to be honest. Relieved that he doesn't have to pay for his soon-to-be ex?? Yeah. Probably.

Sam does make another date to see me next week so I try to tell myself that I am just **mentally** ill. I am still feeling a bit tense, though, after he's gone and I'm glad I've arranged to see Maudie tonight. (Kim's at home visiting her family this weekend.) I give Maudie a quick ring as I **head back** to school and ask her if she wants to meet me in the Kensington common room to listen to the

+++ fragile – zerbrechlich +++ bill – Rechnung +++ lightning – Blitz +++ mental – geistig +++ to head back – zurückgehen +++

new Kitty Gagarins CD. Although she hates Ed, she loves music and she's excited. She can be there at eight.

It's now only six o'clock: I still have two hours to kill. Man, it would be the *perfect* time to go into the darkroom and develop some pictures. I really want to make copies of my White Out pictures. I've found a **decent** camera shop where you can get good black and white **prints**, but it's expensive and, anyway, I love developing myself. That way the pictures are *all mine.*

My legs are on a mission. They carry me to the corridor where the art classrooms are. Oh, **what the heck**! I might just *try* the door of the darkroom and see if it's locked. I mean, it's not like I'm banned from going in there.

The darkroom door *is* locked. I know where the key is, of course, but I can't get it because Miss Shaw's classroom isn't open either at the weekend. Oh well.

Except, as I walk past her room, I notice that there *is* a light on there. I **peer** through the glass in the door and see a young and, sorry Sam Reid, absolutely *hot* looking blond-haired man in his 20s sitting there. The supply teacher! He's checking paint pots at the moment, examining **brushes**.

It's my big chance. I go for it. I knock on the door. I'm friendly. "Hi, Sir," I say, "I'm one of Miss Shaw's students. I'm here for the darkroom key."

The supply teacher stares at me blankly for a moment. He's too handsome to work in an all-girl's

+++ decent – ganz gut +++ print – Papierfoto +++ What the heck! – Was soll's! +++ to peer – gucken +++ brush – Pinsel +++

school, honestly. It's not safe. Perhaps I should warn him. And why can't we have him instead of Miss Bardwell, God? Why???

The Adonis-supply-teacher-guy smiles. He seems relieved that I'm not here to stalk him or something. He introduces himself as, "Mr Radcliffe, taking Miss Shaw's place for a few weeks. You're a photographer?"

I nod. Mr Radcliffe looks around uncertainly. "Well, I *suppose* it's OK for you to have the key. Do you know where it is?"

Do I know? Does the **pope** have a balcony? I go straight over to the blackboard but, naturally, the key which usually hangs there is gone. Miss Bardwell! What did I tell you about her reading my mind? She must have put a tiny computer chip in my brain that tells her exactly what I'm about to do.

There's one part of my mind that she can't get a signal in, it seems. There's a second key, hanging in Miss Shaw's cupboard! That's still there. I grab it quickly and say goodbye to Mr Radcliffe, who's already cutting up pieces of **clay** and who seems to have already forgotten I'm in the room. I'm not anymore anyway.

It's a small victory, but it makes me *sooooo* happy. I run to the dorm to fetch my undeveloped films and spend the next two hours with my bottles and my paper and my pictures – I love it. And I finally get to see my pictures from that night with Sam in White Out. The ones of him with Mrs White are **awesome**! I laugh, I blush.

+++ pope – Papst +++ clay – Ton +++ awesome – großartig +++

He'll love them! When I'm finished, I decide that the safest place for the key is with me. No one else ever comes here anyway. I take it back to the dorm and put it in a drawer with my pictures of lovely, lovely Sam.

Time to meet Maudie. Officially, we're supposed to be helping each other revise for the end-of-term tests we have coming up. But I **suspect** we *might* end up "studying" the music of the Kitty Gagarins a bit more intensively. Oh, and now I remember, I also really have to check if it's OK if I bring Melissa to the Bloomsbury party.

I run into Maudie on the stairs as I'm coming from the darkroom. She's in a good mood, I can tell and I decide to ask her about Melissa straight away. Maudie goes a bit red. "Oh, yes, well, that should be OK. Kim has invited a girl from Knightsbridge that can't come. She still got one ticket spare. She can invite Melissa, I'm sure. I'm bringing you, of course, and, well, I've actually asked *someone else.*" Maudie's red. Suspiciously red.

Someone else, eh? It's a boy, of course! Maudie's got her eye on someone! His name is Rob and he's in the fifth form at St Dougan's. Maudie debated against him once and they've sort of **kept in touch** ever since on Facebook: "Ooh, he's *nice.* You know, not Ed *nice.* Sam *nice.* Oh, and he loves music …"

I don't think she had to tell me that. I'm really pleased for Maudie. It's great that she's into someone new and that she's finally over Ed. Time to celebrate! Time to get the CD out!

+++ to suspect – unterstellen +++ to keep in touch – in Kontakt bleiben +++

Maudie's really excited about hearing it. We have the common room to ourselves – things are quiet this weekend. I stick *Too Cool for School* in the CD player we have, an old one. "Oh, pump it up!" yells Maudie. "They're a great band. I can even forgive them having Ed Stanton on guitar."

Maudie and me then do a lot of stupid dancing, the kind we can't do when Kim's around because she's a *good* dancer. After about half an hour of this, we're on fire. We're totally thirsty and hungry – all that dancing. "Why don't we get a kebab and bring it back here?" I suggest. I'm **starving**: I only had that little bit of Scottish fish with Sam before.

There's a great kebab place just along from St Dougan's, always full of boys (and an amazing place to take them away, or so I've heard). Maudie and me are only picking up food tonight so we're back in under 20 minutes. We're walking along the corridor towards the common room, carrying our bags of food and singing a bit to ourselves when we hear it: *I don't like your rules and we're too cool for school!* Maudie looks at me in surprise. "I thought you switched the CD off."

"I did," I say quickly. My heart sinks. I look at my watch – 8.20. I've suddenly just lost my appetite. Saturday night – *Windswept Love* starts in ten minutes.

+++ to starve – verhungern +++

It Takes a Groupie to Know a Groupie

It is them, of course. DJ Cyclops and her **posse** *rockin' da house.* It's a terrifying sight: Florence and Sienna, the spooky twins, are "dancing" to the Kitty Gagarins track. They look like matching robots on valium. Laurie's there, too, banging into furniture (she can't see it). It's like a scene from a musical disaster movie.

And, **hells bells**, it's the weekend! Don't any of these girls have *homes* to go to? Maudie lives hundreds of miles away from here, so she's got an excuse. Amanda and her crew are all from London or near it – micrometres from here. So what are they doing hanging out at school on Saturday, watching bad TV and annoying me? Their parents must hate them. And right now, I don't **blame** their parents.

"Your CD, Fräulein?" hisses Amanda suddenly. "A little bird told me the band were in the studio this week. Let me guess, Ed Stanton gave it to you?" She knows all about me and Ed, of course. I bet she knows about Ed and Maudie, too. She won't **tease** Maudie, of course – she's still hoping for an invite to the Bloomsbury party. And I don't care, personally. I remember that Amanda

+++ posse – Truppe +++ hells bells – zum Teufel +++ to blame s.o. – jmdm. die Schuld geben +++ to tease – aufziehen +++

was crazy about Ed – she called him her “destiny”. She would have given her good eye to go out with him, but he wasn’t interested.

“The band only has four members,” says Amanda sarcastically. She’s trying really hard to seem not too evil in front of Maudie, I can tell. “It’s not going to take me long to work it out. Let’s see, Steve? Or the drummer, whatsisname, the Scottish one …”

I go over to the CD player and switch it off. The twins scowl at me and – miracle! – one of them actually speaks. “We were listening to that!” **grunts** the-one-standing-on-the-left-of-the-girl-who-looks-exactly-like-her. Sienna?

“Too bad!” I shout. I take the CD out and put it carefully back in its case. I look over at Maudie – she hasn’t said a word yet. She doesn’t like conflict, our Maudie. I’m on my own and I can only mutter, “It’s time for your stupid animal romance show anyway.”

As I say it, Laurie’s face lights up and the twins make an **odd** groaning noise. They both rush over *at exactly the same time* and switch the TV on. Then they sit round it. Ha! *Windswept Love’s* already started. A voice says, “I’m afraid we’ll have to amputate the puppy’s leg.”

Yummy. Maudie and me flee to the Bloomsbury common room, but the evening’s been **ruined**, of course. As I eat my cold kebab, I keep seeing Amanda’s face, busily trying to work out where I got my “exclusive” CD from. There will be trouble if she does find out: it takes a groupie to know a groupie.

+++ to grunt – grummeln +++ odd – komisch +++ to ruin – ruinieren

The rest of the week flies by. I spend most of it ignoring Amanda and working on my essay (on Van Gogh's sunflowers) for Miss Bardwell. I have an allergy to the words "sunshine" and "yellow" by the time I finish it, but still, I do actually finish it. I hand it in to Miss Bardwell with eleven shopping days still to go until Christmas!

Eleven days!!!!! My Christmas shopping has to happen *soon.* The only present I've got so far is Nora's. I bought her a great book about Diane Arbus in a second-hand book shop in Camden I was in the other week. Nora. That heartbreaker. She still hasn't confirmed for the party. *Blame it on Rio.* She's not going to make it, I know it.

Budget crisis time: I have a quick look in the envelope of money that Nora gave me on my first day here. There are 100 pounds left in it. My mum and the Queen Mother have both sent me pre-Christmas "bonuses" of 50 pounds each – that makes 200 pounds. Loads of money – in *Berlin*, the 38th most expensive city in the world. Not very much here, in London, the 3rd most expensive city in the world. But I'll manage. I'm creative.

It's no fun to shop alone, of course. Maudie and Kim want to go at the weekend, too, so that's fine. I e-mail Sam to ask him if he wants to come with us: *Shopping* ***sucks!*** he replies. *Charmant.* He needs to work on the Kitty Gagarins website, which is still not finished, he says. He *says.*

So it's *Ladies Only* that Saturday as we set off down Oxford Street. I love it: the lights, the **prospect of** Christ-

+++ It sucks – Das ist ätzend +++ prospect of – Aussicht auf +++

mas. I even like the fact that English people, normally so polite, become aggressive monsters at this time of year. Everyone is on "Mission Christmas". My personal mission today is to get brilliant things for Mum, Dad, Mad Max, the Queen Mother and Sam.

I spend nearly all of my budget, but I'm pretty happy with what I buy everyone. A Chelsea football shirt for Max, some cool books and English toffees for Mum and Dad, **lavender** soap and Earl Grey teabags for the QM. And Sam's present is a DVD of that old Japanese film we sort of saw at the cinema recently, plus a **frame** to put round a photo of him and Mrs White. He'll love that. I can't wait to give it to him … at the Bloomsbury party, maybe?

+++ lavender – Lavendel +++ frame – Rahmen +++

Santa Claus is coming to Kensingto(w)n

I made a joke before about being able to predict the future, remember? When I knew I was going to trip over Amanda's rug before I actually did? Well, I can tell you this, if I *really* were **psychic** and I had known what would happen to me on the 22nd of December 2008, I would have stayed in bed. With the blankets pulled totally over my head. No, actually, with the blankets ***nailed*** to my head.

In reality, I have no idea what's **in store** for me on "Party Day", of course, so I am – fool! – actually quite excited when I wake up on that fateful morning. It's not every day at Chalk Farm school that you have parties to go to. *And now there are two!!* The Kensington one will be boring, no doubt, but the Bloomsbury one will rock. I can feel it in my water.

Our party is supposed to start around 4 pm. I kill time in the common room, in the study rooms, the library. I keep moving: I'm on the run from Cyclops. She'll be ***desperate*** to find a way into the Bloomsbury party now! So "desperate" that she might kidnap me and

+++ to be psychic – hellseherische Kräfte haben +++ to nail – nageln
+++ to be in store – auf Lager sein +++ desperate – verzweifelt +++

make Maudie and Kim give her a ticket as **ransom**. Cyclops will stop at *nothing*. She'd **sacrifice** the spooky twins to get in, I'm sure of it.

I really hope Melissa hasn't told Cyclops that she's going to the party: that won't help. I managed to whisper my invitation to Melissa secretly last week – she smiled, really smiled, for the first time in ages.

I'm **on edge** all day. I can't take my eyes off my phone. I *still* don't know for sure whether Nora will come this afternoon or not. She will definitely be able to take me to the Queen Mother's for the Christmas holidays tomorrow but she can't promise that she'll make the party.

I'm feeling a bit **low** by the time I finally have to go down to the assembly hall. I take my camera with me. There will be nothing of any interest to photograph at the party, I'm sure. But photos of it will be good evidence in the future of how *spießig* life here at Chalk Farm was. I try to imagine people's shocked faces: *Ja, das haben sie tatsächlich ein "Fest" genannt …*

I spend ages finding my **flashgun** and the party is already "in full swing" when I arrive at half past four. Full swing = lots of desperate people singing *Rudolph the Red Nosed* ***Reindeer*** very quietly. It's depressing, in fact: the assembly hall looks *exactly the same* as it always does. There's just one lonely banner reading "*Merry Christmas Kensington!*" hanging at the back of the stage, in front of which Miss Bardwell and some other teach-

+++ ransom – Lösegeld +++ to sacrifice – opfern +++ to be on edge – nervös sein, gereizt sein +++ low – schwach +++ flashgun – Blitzlichtgerät +++ reindeer – Rentier +++

ers are standing. Mrs Randall, our **headmistress**, famous mainly for her bizarre hats, is there. Today's hat seems to have a dead kangaroo and some **mistletoe** on it. *Tasty*. Mr Benn is there, looking like he's counting the seconds till he can leave.

The assembly hall is half full; most of the girls from our house are here. Most of them look bored already. You'd get more of a *Partystimmung* at one of the Queen Mother's Backgammon evenings.

Interestingly, some girls – *shock!* – actually do have their parents with them! They *exist!* You rarely see anybody's mums or dads here at the school. No one even really talks about them. It's a bit like being in an episode of *Lost*: we're all the survivors of a plane crash at Chalk Farm, with dark secrets we just *don't* want to discuss.

I glance around **curiously**. I see Becks's parents for the first time, **for instance**. Her dad looks like a **posh** weightlifter! Her mum looks like Becks will in 2041! Melissa's parents couldn't come, she told me and I don't see anyone standing with Cyclops – shame!

Then I notice that Miss Bardwell is giving me a **cross** look. I'm late but I'm actually not the last person to arrive. Four people arrive later than me. Ooh, the tension.

The first two latecomers are Olga and a large, handsome, **suntanned** man. He has a powerful aura, the man, the kind of person your eyes *order* you to stare at. He doesn't look much like Olga – he's dark-haired, with

+++ headmistress – Rektorin +++ mistletoe – Mistelzweig +++ curious – neugierig +++ for instance – zum Beispiel +++ posh – piekfein, nobel +++ cross – schräg +++ suntanned – braungebrannt +++

deep brown eyes – but he's holding Olga's hand firmly, in a **possessive** way. Her m/billionaire father?

Olga and her partner take their places in the darkest corner of the room, the area furthest away from the stage. I'm busy trying to get a closer look at Olga's companion when the third late guest arrives.

Nora! In her beautiful Prada coat, the one I pray she'll leave me in her will one day. (I hope she doesn't die any time soon, of course. But still, it is a totally *awesome* coat.) She's carrying her camera case, too! She's looking round for me now and I wave. I'm so excited that I'm actually jumping up and down. I can't believe she's here!

Miss Bardwell can't believe it either. She's helping to line up chairs for the first game when she spots Nora. She starts banging the chairs down just a little bit harder than she did before, I notice.

Nora slips over to join me. "What have I missed?" she whispers. "Absolutely nothing," I **sigh**. I'm so glad she's there. I'm *saved.*

"Right then, ladies," trills Miss Bardwell. "Before we start the fun part of the evening: we have a little business to deal with first. Report cards."

Nightmare. I was hoping she'd forgotten about them. Only a sadist like Miss Bardwell would hand out report cards at a *party.* We all line up, sighing, and Miss Bardwell hands them out to us. We get two copies of our reports, one for us and one for our parents. Miss Bardwell laughs as she gives me my envelopes. It's not a nice laugh.

+++ possessive – besitzergreifend +++ to sigh – seufzen +++

As if that wasn't terrible enough, we then actually *have to* play "**Musical Chairs**". I'm out in the first round – oh no! – but it's terrifying how hard some of the other girls try to win. The final two left in the game are Becks and her friend Babs Deeds, hockey goal-keeper/Cyclops' eye **smasher.** It's like a scene from *Gladiator* when they go for the last chair: Becks elbows Babs in the stomach, but Babs finally **scrambles** onto the chair, pushing her foot into Beck's face. *Sieger*! Her prize for nearly killing herself and her best friend is – *a large bar of Toblerone.* Nora laughs, really loudly, at this which makes me laugh, really loudly, too. Hey, it must be genetic.

Miss Bardwell looks like she wishes we actually were in the Colosseum right now and she could throw Nora and me to the lions. "Emily, if you and your ***relative*** wouldn't **mind** being quiet for one moment, I'd like to introduce a very special guest." And on to the stage comes the fourth person to arrive after me. "Santa."

I have to admit it: just for a moment, I wonder if it *might* be the real thing. But "Santa" is a bit too tall and too thin and it's *definitely* Mr Michaels, the Chemistry teacher from St Dougan's who's been **engaged** to Miss Bardwell for centuries.

As Santa comes onto the stage, waving and shouting: "Ho ho ho!" Miss Bardwell looks like she'll explode with love and pride. Unfortunately, she doesn't explode with

+++ Musical Chairs – Reise nach Jerusalem +++ smasher – Zertrümmerer/in +++ to scramble – krabbeln +++ relative – Verwandte/r +++ to mind – etwas ausmachen +++ engaged – verlobt +++

love or pride or anything else and instead – you may want to be sick now – starts to *flirt* with Santa in a bizarre, creepy way. She ***strokes** his fake beard.*

"Her **fiancé**," I mutter to Nora, but Nora's not there. She's gone off to take a picture of something else in the room – a group of girls laughing, it seems. She's a born photographer, Nora, she can smell a good photo **opportunity**. I sometimes wonder if I will ever be able to do the same.

Santa, meanwhile, is totally getting into character. "Hello, girls!" he booms. "Have you all been good this year?"

And then he opens his sack to **reveal** the world's worst set of Christmas presents. They're *terrible.* Becks, for instance, gets a book called *Hockey for Dummies.* Sadie gets a **comb**, Melissa a jigsaw puzzle of the Taj Mahal. I could go on. To be absolutely fair, I should say that not *all* the presents today are cheap and boring. One girl's present is actually really, really nice.

"Amanda?" says Santa and Cyclops walks towards him. She looks very relaxed. As everyone watches her **tear** the paper off her present, I suddenly realise – *she knows what's inside already.*

"Oh wow! Just the one I had my eye on. Cashmere!" she squeals. It's a beautiful scarf, a truly nice, expensive-looking one. She slips it around her neck. It's gorgeous, though I hate to say it. Amanda then actually kisses *both* "Santa" and "**Bride** of Santa" on the cheek.

+++ to stroke – streicheln +++ fiancé – Verlobte/r +++ opportunity – Gelegenheit +++ to reveal – enthüllen +++ comb – Kamm +++ to tear – reißen +++ bride – Braut +++

It's no accident that this was the scarf Amanda "had her eye on", of course. Amanda was, it's clear, Miss Bardwell's "personal shopper". And Amanda's budget for Christmas presents obviously looked something like this: *Total Kensington Christmas Present* ***fund****: 200 pounds, Amanda's present – 150 pounds, presents for all other Unmenschen in Kensington – 50 pounds.*

A voice says, "Emily?" Santa's grinning at me. I'm up.

My first thought when I have my Christmas present in my hands is: *thank goodness!* I can tell from the shape that it's obviously a book and so not deodorant or **wart** cream or something. I open it up nervously and then stare at the cover: *English-German Dictionary For Beginners.* There's a picture of a cat and the words *Katze = cat* next to it. And a picture of a dog and, oh, you **get** the idea.

It's not even *funny.* Kindergarten children know this stuff. I've been speaking English since I was *born.* I can hear Amanda laughing and she actually says, loud and clear, "Wunderbar!" She hasn't even seen the cover. She doesn't have to. She chose it for me.

I'll kill her, I think as I walk down the steps from the stage. It will be my Christmas present to the world – a Cyclops-free New Year! But just a second later I've forgotten all about getting a stupid dictionary …

Olga's been called up to get her **gift**. She finally comes out of the shadows. Everyone, even Cyclops, falls silent. All eyes are on Olga, who's so beautiful, so blonde, she

+++ fund – Budget +++ wart – Warze +++ to get – *hier:* verstehen +++ gift – Geschenk +++

seems to glow. Her companion stays hidden in the shadows, I notice.

Olga takes her present silently from Santa and opens it slowly. It's a mirror, a cheap, pink plastic one. Olga stares at her own reflection in it for a moment. She looks like a **doomed** princess in a fairy tale, one who just *knows* she's not going be living happily after.

I can't help it. It's probably not the right thing to do, but Olga looks so gorgeous – I raise my camera: *Pow! Pow!* There are two flashes: Nora takes a picture at *exactly* the same time as me. We're like a couple of paparazzi.

The flashes from our cameras seem to break Olga's private **spell**. She lifts her head, looks around the room, and says in a quiet voice, "Thanks for the lovely present. I'd also like to say thanks to everyone for everything. This will be my last term here. I'm going back to school in Florida after Christmas."

It's as if Olga has just thrown a hand grenade into the room. Everyone gasps. Miss Bardwell squeals and seems to be about to have a panic attack. She loves rich parents and they don't come much richer than Olga's, of course. Mr Benn looks really sad, Mrs Randall just looks confused and plays nervously with her hat. And then there's Melissa. She's staring at Olga in shock.

Olga's not looking at anyone anymore. Head down, mirror in hand, she goes back over to the dark-haired man. He puts her arm around her and they leave the assembly hall.

+++ doomed – verloren +++ spell – Bann +++

I Saw Auntie Kissing Santa Claus

I'm just about to say something to Nora when I notice that Nora, actually, doesn't seem very interested in Olga. She does, however, appear to be absolutely fascinated by *Santa.*

She's staring at him in a funny way, turning her head to the side as though he were an **upside down** painting or something. "Who *is* that in the suit?" she whispers finally. "There's something *very* familiar about him."

I didn't get a chance to tell her before, I realise: "It's Mr Michaels, Miss Bardwell's fiancé! They've been engaged for, like, eleven years! He teaches Chemistry at St Dougan's and …"

I talk some more but Nora says nothing. I can tell she's surprised. It's true. Someone who finds Miss Bardwell attractive – it is, truly, *amazing.* But it's more than that, it seems.

"Excuse me a moment," Nora mutters softly. She heads towards the stage and climbs the steps to where Santa and Miss Bardwell are standing. They're obviously talking about Olga – Miss Bardwell is **flapping** her arms around, looking like a stressed-out **raven.**

+++ upside down – auf dem Kopf hängend +++ to flap – flattern +++ raven – Rabe +++

After that, it's as if I'm watching a very strange theatre play. I see my aunt go over to Miss Bardwell and shake her hand, then turn to Santa, whisper something in his ear and kiss him on the mouth! Just like that. Santa looks like he can't believe it and Miss Bardwell has just gone as white as "Santa's beard".

Nora smiles again, a bit sadly, then turns and walks down the steps. When she reaches me, before I can ask her anything, she says, "Come on, let's **get lost**. The party's over, I have the feeling."

Off we go, leaving behind a room full of breathless Kensington girls, unable to believe that what should have been the world's most boring party has actually been so *dramatic*.

+++ to get lost – abhauen +++

We're outside and it feels nice, cold though it is. The assembly hall was hot and tense, and the night breeze is a wonderful change. Phew! What was all that *kissing Santa* about?

I don't have a jacket with me and Nora takes off her beautiful coat and gives me that to wear. It's too big but feels lovely. "We'll just find a café," says Nora a bit dreamily. She smiles. "Then I'll explain."

We go to White Out, which is **packed**, full of noisy, **merry** people eating their Christmas chips. Nora tells me that there was a café here in "her day" but it was called the Golden Tulip Café back then. "It was full of plants. Definitely no boxing posters."

We sit down and I wait. Not for my chips or my tea or Mrs White to come **shuffling** over, as usual. I need an answer to the evening's burning question: How does Nora know Santa, I mean, Mr Michaels?

Nora doesn't make me wait long. "I used to sit with him here, back when it was the Golden Tulip Café."

I blink. *With him?*

"With Ben," Nora says quietly, staring hard at the menu board behind the counter. "Ben Michaels. He's the one I told you about when you were upset about that boy. The one who broke my heart with a "Dear Jane" letter? Ben was a pupil at St Dougan's then. I haven't seen him since. I had no idea that he was a teacher there or that …"

Or that he was engaged to Cruella de Bardwell. It can't be true. It *can't* be. Nora told me about her "Dear Jane"

+++ packed – voll +++ merry – fröhlich +++ to shuffle – schlurfen +++

letter when I'd just been dumped by text by Ed. The same person who dropped Nora – beautiful, clever, funny Nora – is now with *Miss Bardwell* – ugly, boring, nasty Miss Bardwell. It's official – all men really are *mad.*

Nora's smiling. "I'm pretty sure he didn't leave me for Connie Bardwell, if that's what you're thinking. Connie didn't have much luck with the boys back then. She had problems with her teeth."

And her face, I think bitterly. And her personality. And her … I could go on until next Christmas.

Nora says quickly, "They must have met up later, the last two survivors of St Dougan's and Chalk Farm School."

A young waitress has just come over – there's no sign of either Mr or Mrs White tonight – and we're just about to order when I hear someone shout, "Look who's here! It's Santa, everyone." And it seems as though the whole café turns to stare.

What a sight. Santa, **aka** Mr Michaels, is standing in the doorway, his beard half-falling off his face. Everyone laughs and a couple of people call out things like: "Where's my present?" But Santa hasn't got any presents with him this time. From the look on his face, he *has* brought a lot of unfinished business with him.

And Santa's a stalker! He must have followed us here. I try to imagine Miss Bardwell's face as she watched him leave and I get a warm feeling all over my body. If only

+++ aka – alias +++

I could have seen it – it would have been the best Christmas present. Ever.

Ben/Santa/Mr Michaels comes straight over to our table. "I was sure I'd find you here, Nora and emm …" He stares at me, blankly and scratches his beard. The waitress who's still waiting for our order looks just a little bit frightened of him.

"This is Emily, my **niece**," says Nora calmly. If she's surprised to see him, she doesn't show it. "Will you be joining us for some tea and some chips? And Ben? Maybe you could take off the beard?"

Mr Michaels nods and blushes, quickly taking off his beard and hat and putting them on the table. He's still out of breath – he must have run all the way here. He can't stop gazing at Nora. "20 years," he mutters. Our waitress rolls her eyes and disappears.

It's the first time I've seen Mr Michaels up close. He's not *exactly* handsome, but he is actually quite a pleasant looking man, with a kind face. His dark hair is standing up everywhere, though, from having been under his Santa hat for *four hours.* That's probably why he scared our waitress.

He's noticed that I'm looking at him: he looks back. "You're Eleanor's daughter," he says in a soft voice. "You're not really like her."

Eleanor is my mum and she's blonde and small and beautiful. So no, I'm nothing like her.

Nora smiles. "Emily's like her dad. Eleanor married an East German writer from Berlin."

+++ niece – Nichte +++

An East German writer from Berlin! It makes my dad sound really exciting and exotic, when he's *soooo* not! But Mr Michaels looks impressed. "Eleanor was always so quiet. You were the rebel, Nora."

Before things can get any more nostalgic/intense, cups of teas and chips arrive. I'm the only one who's going to eat or drink anything, I'm sure of it. This is all too strange, it really is. Here I am in a café with the fiancé of my **archenemy**, who also happens to be Sam's chemistry teacher and an old flame of my aunt's. Oh, *why* can't Sam's phone be working?? This is hot stuff. I would love to text him.

As I eat my chips, I'm starting to get the feeling my aunt and her old flame would rather be alone right now. It's nearly time for me to get ready for round 2 anyway. The real party of the night: Bloomsbury's. I find myself almost hoping that that will be a bit boring. I've had enough excitement!

I clear my plate quickly – pretty easy – and say goodnight to Nora and Mr Michaels. Nora will pick me up at around ten tomorrow to drive to Grandma's. "So don't be too late in bed!" As I leave, I can't help it: I look back at Nora and Mr Michaels through the window of White Out. I see Mr Michaels reach out for Nora's hand. He doesn't get it. Her hand stays where it is, holding her coffee cup.

Man, Nora's *cool.* Respect.

+++ archenemy – Erzfeind/in +++

The Party from Hell

I only have time now to fly back to the dorm, quickly change into the red dress that I bought for the Kitty Gagarins concert and pull a brush through my hair. Then I grab my Christmas present for Sam, stick it in my bag and head down to the main hall to meet Melissa. She gives me a quick summary of what I missed after the Kensington party: No one, not even Josh it seems, really knows why Olga's leaving. And yes, the look on Miss Bardwell's face was *priceless* when Mr Michaels left the room.

Melissa's curious, of course, about my aunt and Mr Michaels, but I just mumble something quickly about Nora and him *being at school together.* Melissa nods – her mind's on the next party now, luckily.

Even just **approaching** the assembly hall it's clear: this party is **the real deal**. It even has its own *Türsteher*, a mean-looking fifth-form girl named Dorothy. She's carefully checking names off on the guest list. Luckily, Mrs McKee did remember to add Melissa's and – hurrah! – we're in.

It's amazing. It's like being a different room. It's hard

+++ to approach – sich nähern +++ the real deal – der Hammer +++

to believe that just a few hours ago there were girls playing *Musical Chairs* here. Now instead there are people standing around, probably chatting about Damien Hirst or Swedish electro-pop or something.

There's actually some cool electro-pop playing now – why it's DJ Maudie, of course! She waves to me from behind a stereo system that's been set up on the stage. She doesn't seem as happy as she should, somehow. Maybe she has technical problems. I wonder if Rob is here yet.

And where's Kim? I finally spot her talking to an attractive woman who looks like the kind of art student/actress you find wandering around *Prenzlauer Berg* where I live in Berlin, but who I think is actually Mrs McKee. Kim mouths: *Be with you in a minute.*

Over there are the boys – a hot and hopeful looking group of them. I don't think they can believe they've actually made it in here, girl heaven. It's all so nearly perfect. All I need now is for one of the boys to be Sam and then my happiness will be complete. It's great in Bloomsbury. *Great.*

Then the roof falls in on everything. *I see her.* Talking to a hot and hopeful looking guy in a grey **jumper** and jeans. *Cyclops.* She's wearing a white dress, **teamed with** a totally *bling bling* pair of gold and **amber** sunglasses and a gold **necklace**. She looks like she's just got off P-Diddy's yacht. It's a very un-Bloomsbury kind of look.

It can't be true! She wasn't invited. She *wasn't.* She

+++ jumper – Pullover +++ teamed with – gepaart mit +++ amber – Bernstein +++ necklace – Halskette +++

doesn't have any friends in Bloomsbury, I'm certain of it. Maybe she used chloroform on Dorothy the **bouncer** or …

It's just then, at *exactly* the wrong moment, that Sam arrives, looking nervous and a little annoyed. He waves over at me. It's stupid, but I can't help it: I ignore him. Cyclops has spotted both Sam and me now, too, and her face lights up. She's watching us. If she really does make the connection between us, she'll spoil everything, I'm sure of it.

My evening's officially ruined. There will be no dancing with Sam and getting **cosy** with him later. Instead I'm going to have to spend the whole night **pretending** he's some kind of boring stranger with a **disease**, who wants to sell me a bible.

Kim comes over. "Have you seen her?" she asks **anxiously**. "Maudie's not happy either. Amanda's been talking to Rob since she got here. You know Rob, the guy Maudie likes."

Brilliant. So Cyclops is going to destroy Maudie's evening, too. I look over at the music deck and, sure enough, Maudie is now gazing miserably at Amanda, who's actually feeling Rob's arm and squealing: "Ooh! Big muscles, baby. Got any more like those?" *Ugghhhh!* Or as they say back home: *Eeeeeeeeee!*

I *hate* to say I told Maudie so – correction, I *really* hate to say I told Maudie so – but I did. Cyclops is the ***devil***. Maudie's just found that out the hard way.

+++ bouncer – Rausschmeißer/in +++ cosy – gemütlich +++ to pretend – so tun als ob +++ disease – Krankheit +++ anxious – besorgt +++ devil – Teufel +++

I look over nervously at Sam again. He's confused: all my crazy nodding in the direction of Amanda isn't helping. I suddenly realise that though Sam has heard me talk about Cyclops, he's never seen her before. He can't understand why I'm not talking to him. He finally just shrugs his shoulders and heads for the buffet set up on several long tables at the side of the hall.

It gives me a good opportunity to explain things to him. I glance at Cyclops, who's still flirting heavily with Rob, and queue up behind Sam at the buffet. I pretend to examine a rather nice looking salsa salad and lean over and whisper in his ear: "Cyclops is here. Amanda. She's trouble. I just thought we'd better play it cool."

Sam doesn't look at me. Instead he puts four cocktail sausages on his plate, thinks for a moment, then adds a fifth. He *is* in a bad mood, I can tell. "I'll just eat this and go home then, shall I?" he mumbles, grabbing *two* muffins. "I don't feel like playing games tonight. Not even *cool* ones."

Sam finally turns to face me. Now that we're standing next to each other, he actually looks more worried than angry. Something *is* wrong. Oh, I get it. He wants to break up, but he's too nice to do it to me so soon after Ed, so near to Christmas. I suddenly remember my present for him in my bag and blush.

"What's up?" I say. My voice sounds flat, even to me. My heart *hurts*.

"I don't want to talk about it," Sam snaps. "I'm going to find somewhere to sit and eat this. Then I think I'll go and finish my packing. *Great* party by the way. Thanks for the invite!" And he's gone.

Sam's not the only one who wants to leave: It's 9.48 pm on the night of what *should have been* the party of the year and I'm already thinking about going, too. I'm tired and the situation with Sam is horrible. I'm desperate to talk to him, but every time I move anywhere near him, I can feel Amanda's **dodgy** eyes boring holes in my back. She's probably been sent by Miss Bardwell on some kind of spying mission!

Bingo! I'm right and it's Kim who **confirms** it when we meet a few minutes later for "crisis update talks": "Miss Bardwell got Amanda in to the party! She **blackmailed** Mrs McKee … told her that Amanda has special needs!"

Special needs again, eh? Right now, I'd say Amanda *specially needs* a **punch** in the face. I look around me – Sam sitting eating in a corner, lonely and bored, Maudie staring at Rob, looking **heartsick**. Amanda's the only one with a smile on her face. She's grinning and clapping her hands at something Rob's saying. *Merry Christmas everybody, lots of love from Miss Bardwell!*

And – oh no! – even *Melissa* seems to be having a bad time. She's talking to one of the St Dougans' boys: it's Josh, her brother! Oh my! It looks like an intense and depressing talk: Josh has his head in his hands. Let me guess – Olga. Josh must be heartbroken about her leaving, of course. Man, this is a *nightmare* party! An "Alcoholics Anonymous" meeting would have more laughs.

It seems as though Kim is now trying to rescue some-

+++ dodgy – *hier:* hinterhältig +++ to confirm – bestätigen +++ to blackmail – erpressen +++ punch – Schlag +++ heartsick – tief betrübt +++

thing from the evening. She's up dancing – she looks amazing, totally elegant and cool at the same time. I think she wants to support Maudie, too, and to show her what a great DJ she is.

That's what I should be doing! I stop staring at Sam, who is *still* eating and *still* sitting by himself, and get up on the dance floor to join Kim. It's really fun. We wave at Maudie and shake our **fists** in the direction of Cyclops. I actually relax for five minutes.

It's a fatal tactical error. When I look up, just to see Sam's face again, I can't believe it. He's still sitting in the same corner of the room. But he's stopped eating now and no longer has a plate of food on his knee. Sitting on his knee instead is Cyclops Dobson.

+++ fist – Faust +++

Amanda has her arms around Sam's neck, but she's facing me. She looks like the cat that got the **cream**, as my grandmother would say. The cat that's got *my* cream! Sam just looks shocked and helpless.

I'm off the dance floor and standing next to them faster than you can say: *put my boyfriend down!* I'm furious. ***Raging*** *bull.* I snort. But Amanda just laughs. "Emily, have you two met? Sam, Emily. Emily, Sam."

"Yeah, we know each other," I growl. Sam looks frozen with terror. I'm sure he wants Cyclops to get off him. He must do, mustn't he? But instead of doing something, he's just blushing. He can't speak. Oh, Sam is so *weak* sometimes!

"There were no seats free," says Amanda, giggling. "So I asked Sam if he would mind me sitting here. He's been such a gentleman."

"I thought you meant *there*," mutters Sam, nodding towards a small space next to him. "Would you mind …?" He shuffles under her.

Amanda ignores the signal. "And I had no idea I was *sitting on someone famous*! Sam's the drummer from the Kitty Gagarins, Emily. I'm such a big fan! You like their music, too, don't you?" *She knows. She knows.*

Well, if she does really know, there's no point in being **secretive** anymore. "Want to dance, Sam?" I say boldly. Fight fire with fire.

Sam nods eagerly but the reality is – he's **trapped**. Amanda's a tall girl and she doesn't look like she's going *anywhere.*

+++ cream – Sahne +++ raging – rasend +++ secretive – geheimnisvoll +++ trapped – in der Falle +++

"But it's *soooooo* comfortable here," she whispers, in a stupid little girl voice. "And my eye is really sore. Just give me a minute."

A minute! We'll have to call the fire brigade to free Sam!

What should I do? My brain panics, then pulls itself together and presents the following strategies:

Plan A) Scream with ***anger*** *and become Jackie Chan/Lara Croft. Karate* ***chop*** *Cyclops in the face, throw Sam over my shoulder and run. Take him to* ***sanctuary****, give him his Christmas present, kiss him and kiss him and kiss him.*

Plan B) Smile in a cool way, throw head back and return to dance floor. Act like you don't care what Amanda and Sam are doing in the corner. Dance alone for a while. ***Yawn*** *and say goodnight to everyone. Cry like a hundred hungry babies when you get back to the dorm.*

+++ anger – Wut +++ to chop – schlagen +++ sanctuary – Unterschlupf, Zufluchtsort +++ to yawn – gähnen +++

One Last Goodbye

"Plan B", you'll be pleased to hear, is a total success. After I've walked away from Sam and Amanda, thrown my head back, danced with Kim again, acted like I didn't care and yawned, I say goodnight to everyone. Not everyone – I don't even look at the "lovebirds" in the corner. I can't.

I get back to the dorm and carry out the second part of the plan. I cry like a hundred hungry babies, just staring at Sam's Christmas present. I **modify** "Plan B" slightly by adding something to it – I throw my dictionary, *my* stupid Christmas present from those ***witches***, into the **bin** near my bed.

I didn't actually ever think "Plan B" would work so well, of course. Not in my wildest dreams. I was so sure that Sam would finally get Amanda off him and follow me when I left. He didn't. He didn't even *try*.

The morning after the night before. Waking up on the 23rd of December is a horrible experience. For a second, there's a tiny bit of hope that everything that happened

+++ to modify – abändern +++ witch – Hexe +++ bin – Abfalleimer +++

was all a crazy ugly dream. Maybe *today* is actually the day of the parties and everything will go to plan.

Then I see my dictionary for two-year-olds sticking out of the bin. I sigh. It did happen – all of it. Sam and Cyclops. I can't think about it. Instead I'll think about the good news about today really being today: right now, my parents and my brother will be getting on a plane in Berlin. They'll arrive in England soon. I'll leave for The Grange – my grandma's house – around 10.00 and *escape.*

The bad news is, of course, that Sam is also leaving for Scotland today. I won't see him again till January. *Next year.* If I *ever* see him again. I'm probably single once more. I can't even text him. Like I said, I *can't think about it.*

Amanda is still asleep, mouth open, mask on. I used to think that I hated Katharina Müller, my *Erzfeind* back at my old school in Berlin, the Hermann-Hesse Gymnasium. I knew nothing, I realise. Amanda makes Katharina Müller look like Heidi.

Becks is also **unconscious** (she was out with the hockey girls last night, I remember now). It seems as if Melissa's waking up – *brilliant.* I need to talk to someone about what happened at the party after I left. **Urgently**.

I'm just trying to get Melissa's attention when I hear a tiny **rustling** noise. I turn towards the noise and *a note appears under the dormitory door.*

+++ unconscious – bewusstlos +++ urgent – dringend +++ rustling – raschelnd +++

Has this ever happened to you? A letter appearing under a door? It's actually a *really* strange thing to watch: a green envelope with the word *Emily* written on it slides into the dorm.

I go to pick it up. Well, wouldn't you? The handwriting looks familiar … it's Olga's! I know it well from when I once copied, sorry, *borrowed* her essay. I open the envelope:

Emily, I'm in computer room 4. Try and get Melissa to come with you. Please. Olga

As **cryptic** as ever. Olga's too scared to ask Melissa herself, too scared she'll say no, probably.

I look over at Melissa. She's noticed me picking up the note, of course, and I show it to her straight away. I don't want to trick or trap her. She stares at it blankly at first, before finally saying, calmly, "I was wondering if I'd see her again."

Then she looks annoyed. "Olga's so *dramatic*. Why didn't she just text you? Why didn't she just ask me? Oh, never mind. Computer room 4 it is."

Melissa puts on her **dressing gown** and reaches into the drawer of her bedside table to pull out – the 8 x 10 inch **glossy enlargement**! The photo of Josh that Olga "borrowed" from Melissa. Melissa blamed Becks for taking the picture and **World War Three** followed, as well as the end of Melissa and Olga's friendship.

Melissa smiles at me drily: "A going away present."

+++ cryptic – geheimnisvoll +++ dressing gown – Morgenmantel +++ glossy – glänzend +++ enlargement – Vergrößerung +++ World War Three – der Dritte Weltkrieg +++

Melissa's a smart girl. She senses that there's something else that I want to talk about before we see Olga. She doesn't officially know about Sam and me but, of course, she sort of does. "Amanda really had her claws into Sam last night, didn't she? But he wasn't interested, you could see that! She finally gave up with him and went back to flirting with Rob. She's *terrible*."

Hmmm. I can't help but think that if Sam had *really* been having a bad time, he could have got rid of Amanda. And if he'd *really* wanted to follow me, he could have done.

We're at computer room 4. Melissa hesitates, just for a second, then pulls her dressing gown tightly round her and opens the door.

Olga's waiting for us, of course. She's standing in her coat, obviously ready to leave Chalk Farm School for Girls. When she sees us both come in, she's definitely relieved. For a moment Olga and Melissa look at each other. Then an absolutely bizarre thing happens: Olga totally loses her cool and bursts into tears. Olga's manipulative, no question, but I'm sure that right now her heart really is breaking.

Melissa hesitates again for a moment and then goes over and puts her arm round Olga. She strokes her hair. It's probably the same way she strokes Almond's mane; it's a tiny bit *rough*. Then she says, more gently, "Is your father making you leave school?"

Olga nods. "Yes, but that wasn't him last night at the party. That's my Uncle Dimitri. My father's brother. My father sent him to collect me. He's waiting downstairs. I've only got ten more minutes."

"And … why?" I ask. Olga once told me that her father loved England.

Melissa knows the answer. "It's Josh, isn't it? I spoke to him last night and he told me *something* about what's going on."

Olga gazes out of the window. That's how I'll always remember Olga, actually – looking into the distance, transporting herself somewhere else. For the first time I have the feeling that she would really rather be here with us in snowy England than on her way back to America.

Then she speaks. She tells us something of what's been going on in her life since she left dorm 3B. It's not been easy. Olga is nearly 15 and she tells us she's already "engaged" – to a boy called Taki.

"He's the son of my father's business **associate**. I'm not in love with him; it's basically a power alliance," says Olga bitterly. "I don't really have a choice …"

"But you're too young." I begin and Olga just laughs. It's the kind of laugh that a Tsar might have laughed as he chopped a **peasant's** head off or something.

"Oh, I can get married in spring when I turn 16 if I have 93 dollars for a licence and my parents agree. And they do agree." Olga's still talking fast. She doesn't have much time left. It's all really complicated, especially when you're tired and haven't had breakfast and you haven't had anything to eat since half a "heartbreak sausage" at the party from hell. "I had to finish things with Taki – he kept wanting to come over here and I really love Josh, Melissa, I do. So I told Taki it was over and he went to my dad, who freaked out. Then he said I had to come back to the States and *get in line*."

"But Olga," I say, "this is awful. You can't get *married*!! You have to …"

Suddenly I see a flash of the old Olga, sarcastic. "I have to … *what*, Emily? Tell my father where to go? Do you have any idea what my father would do to me if I did?"

I don't have any idea, of course. I don't think I want to. I think of my own dad – so gentle, so funny, so disorganized and so poor – and realize how lucky I am that he's not a billionaire Russian control freak.

Suddenly I have exactly the same feeling that I had the other day with Nora and Mr Michaels – as they say here,

+++ associate – Partner/in +++ peasant – Bauer +++

two's company, three's a crowd. It's clear that Melissa and Olga have a lot to talk about and very little time. I'm out of here. Again.

+++ two's company, three's a crowd – drei sind einer zu viel +++

Ein Herz für Weihnachten

It's a cliché, of course: *Poor little rich girl.* Olga is going back to a life of privilege and sunshine and absolutely no freedom, it seems. Like a really sunny Siberia. I remember what Mr Benn said to me, not so long ago: *Olga's a survivor.* I really hope he's right.

I've had enough now, I need to get totally out of here. My mum and dad and Max will be landing in England in an hour and all I want is to see them. Talk German! Relax! Sleep! Think! That all seems much more exciting than an overdose of drama and intrigue, suddenly.

I sneak into the dorm, praying that Amanda will have gone to breakfast by now: she has. So I pack quickly, all my presents for everyone. My present for Sam. I'd framed that picture and everything. It's not fair. I stare at it for a moment. I can't stop staring at it. I still can't believe the way we left each other last night. I still can't believe that I won't get a chance to give him his gift and wish him Happy Christmas! Kiss him goodbye. How could everything have gone so wrong? How? I must not cry, I must not cry.

I *hate* Cyclops. I hate myself for hating her. If I didn't hate her so much, then maybe I wouldn't worry about her so much. If I hadn't worried so much, then maybe I would have just ignored her at the party and kissed Sam and had a good time and *everything would have been fine.*

I throw Sam's present into my bag – oops! what is still technically my friend Merle's bag – and then **drag** it downstairs. I'm to wait for Nora in front of the school. I hope I don't have to wait too long. We don't just share a love of photography, Nora and me. We also have a shared tendency to be late. I stand near a couple of other girls also waiting for family members to pick them up. I keep my eyes fixed on the drive – Nora has a car you can't miss, a **vintage** 1973 Citroën.

While I'm waiting, I get two texts, one from Maudie – *You were right. Cyclops =* ***bitch*** *from hell. Merry Christmas!* And one from Melissa: *No idea if any of what Olga said is true. Have nice hols!*

Lots to talk about next term, eh? But there's still no word from Sam. I can't believe that he isn't even planning to explain what happened last night. Is this really how it ends? With *nothing*, me never hearing from him again? It's almost worse than what happened with Ed, I think miserably. At least Ed told me that *things weren't working.* At least he took the time to dump me by text. Just knowing what Sam was thinking would be *amazing* right now. *I will be getting married to Cyclops in spring,* for instance. The silence is killing me.

I'm still waiting. Everyone I started out standing with has been picked up by now – *everyone.* Where is Nora? This is just *too* depressing. You can see St Dougan's, for

+++ to drag – schleifen +++ vintage – retro +++ bitch – Miststück +++

one thing. I watch lots of taxis come and go from there. Lots of boys with big rucksacks walk down the path towards freedom and the holidays. I try not to think that Sam might be one of them. *Oh hurry up, Nora!*

Most of the cars leaving the St Dougan's **drive** are either black London city cabs or Audis or Mercedes – hurrah for German technology! One of the cars leaving St Dougan's now stands out from the crowd, however. It is – no question! – *definitely* a 1973 Citroën. Auntie Nora's car.

It can't be! It is! Auntie Nora leaving St Dougan's *first thing in the morning*! Mr Michaels is a housemaster and so lives in the school. Oh, Nora *can't* have spent the night there. She can, of course. She's an adult. She's single. Santa was hot for her.

Santa *isn't* single, though! Not this one. I look around in panic. If my aunt is now officially having an affair with Miss Bardwell's fiancé, then I might as well fly back to Berlin now. I'm not brave enough to stay on at school here if that's what's really happening. Miss Bardwell would take me out into a field and tie me to a tree and leave me there if she found out.

Nora's car is now pulling up in *our* drive. I run outside. *Oh please, let Miss Bardwell not have seen her!* Nora **winds** her window **down** and says calmly, "Hi, sorry, I'm late. The traffic was terrible."

I give her a suspicious look and she stares back at me, amused. Then she starts to really giggle. "Honest,

+++ drive – Auffahrt +++ to wind down – herunterkurbeln +++

mum," she says. "I just had to drop something off at St Dougan's first. A little Christmas present. Ben asked to see some of my photos. You didn't *really* think I'd spent the night there."

"Let's just get out of here," I mutter, looking over my shoulder uneasily. Miss Bardwell might have placed **snipers** in the towers. Thank goodness this isn't a **convertible.**

I go quickly to the back of Nora's car and open the **boot** to put in my case. This, I know, will take around 45 seconds. After that, I'll get into Nora's car and Nora will drive off and *I won't have seen Sam.* I won't even know how to get in touch with him. I don't have a number for his parents in Scotland and his mobile is still broken. Or "broken".

I won't even have been able to have given him his present. Christmas is cancelled. Santa's on strike.

Except – it's not. He isn't. Here's a warning – if you don't like those sentimental films they always show on ZDF around the 23rd of December, which have titles like: *Ein Herz für Weihnachten* or *Liebe über Weihnachten* or something and that your mother watches with a glass of *Weißweinschorle*, then don't read what happens next. You'll hate it. If on the other hand, you're a bit like me and you secretly *love it* when things turn out right, just when they should, then here's what happened after I closed the boot of Nora's car.

+++ sniper – Scharfschütze/-schützin +++ convertible – Cabrio +++ boot – Kofferraum +++

I hear Nora say, "She's round the back." I look up and I can just see Sam, looking breathless and bending down to talk to Nora through her car window.

He stares at me for a moment. He looks **awkward**. "I thought I saw you standing here, then you **vanished**. I should wear my glasses instead of leaving them in my jacket pocket so often." Nora winds the window of her car up.

I'm **stunned**. Talk about last minute! All I can think to say to Sam is, "You're not supposed to be here," which he isn't. The party's over, it's *no boys allowed* here at Chalk Farm again. He shrugs his shoulders. "It's Christmas, who's going to throw me out?"

+++ awkward – unbehaglich +++ to vanish – verschwinden +++ stunned – perplex, fassungslos +++

Sam's holding out a small – actually quite badly **wrapped**, sorry – present that looks like, well, a book. He has a huge rucksack with him, I see now, and he's placed that on the frosty ground.

I don't move. Sam's still holding out the present. "I came here to give you this," he says quietly. "And well, I wanted to explain …"

Suddenly I grab a) the present, then b) Sam and pull him round the back of the school. I know exactly where I'm going: there's an old shed, we can hide behind there.

We make it, we're out of sight. Before you can say, "*Liebe über Weihnachten*", Sam and me are hugging. And then, suddenly, wouldn't you know it – we're kissing. Go ahead and *sue me, Miss Bardwell. Sue me.*

Sam breaks away first. He holds me close, strokes my hair for a second and then says quietly, "I thought you might already have gone. I've only got five minutes before I have to run to catch my bus. I just wanted to say what I hope you already know – that Cyclops girl's a nightmare. That was the worst half an hour of my life sitting under her."

Could it be? Is that a man in a red suit with a white beard, standing behind one of those **oak trees** near us? The one winking at me? No, it couldn't.

"It was me that ruined everything," I mumble. "I should have just ignored her."

Sam smiles. I think he would like to agree but he's too nice. He smiles and then gives me a sort of friendly

+++ to wrap – einpacken +++ oak tree – Eiche

punch in the arm, which actually hurts a bit. "You idiot," he says tenderly. Then he kisses me again.

And just like a truly bad TV movie, that's where this particular school year ends, with angels singing, reindeers crying and idiots kissing. Merry Christmas one and all!

Bei Thienemann von Joanna Thompson in der Reihe "Freche Mädchen – Easy English!" ebenfalls erschienen:

Girls' School – *England Calling*
Girls' School – *The Ed Affair*
Girls' School – *Stand by your Sam*

Thompson, Joanna:
Girls' School – Season of Love
ISBN 978 3 522 50087 6

Reihengestaltung und Gesamtausstattung: Birgit Schössow
Innentypografie: Marlis Killermann
Schrift: Minion und LTT Tapeside
Satz: KCS GmbH, Buchholz/Hamburg
Reproduktion: Medienfabrik, Stuttgart
Druck und Bindung: Friedrich Pustet, Regensburg

5 4 3 2 1° 09 10 11 12

www.thienemann.de
www.frechemaedchen.de